The Visitation

An Overview of the New Testament: Part One

Bob Evely

To Jill

The wife of my youth.
My best friend.
Most definitely my better half.
An amazing wife, mother, and grandma.

You have made this spiritual journey with me,
Every step of the way.

You have always supported me in all that I do.

I appreciate you far more
than words could possibly express.

With love,

Bob

"The Visitation"
Elinor Evely

An Overview of the New Testament: Part One

𝕿𝖍𝖊 𝖁𝖎𝖘𝖎𝖙𝖆𝖙𝖎𝖔𝖓

"The Visitation"

Matthew
Mark
Luke
John

"You knew not the era of your visitation" (Luke 19:44)

Bob Evely.

Copyright 2018, Robert W. Evely, Wilmore KY

*Scriptures taken from the Concordant Literal New Testament
and the Concordant Version of the Old Testament unless otherwise noted.
Concordant Publishing Concern, 15570 West Knochaven Road,
Santa Clarita, CA 91387 (www.Concordant.org)*

Grace Evangel Fellowship:
P O Box 6, Wilmore, KY 40390
www.GraceEvangel.org

The Visitation; An Overview of the New Testament – Part One
by Bob Evely
Copyright © 2018 by Robert W. Evely

All rights reserved. This book or any portion thereof may not be reproduced or used in any manner whatsoever without the express written permission of the publisher except for the use of brief quotations in a book review or scholarly journal.

First Printing: 2018

ISBN 978-1-7323228-6-8

Cover created by Cris Evely
Front: Alex Evely
Back: Drawing by Allison Evely

Published by:
Robert W. Evely
P.O. Box 6
Wilmore, KY 40390

www.GraceEvangel.org

Table of Contents

Introduction	5
Matthew	13
Mark	59
Luke	81
John	121
Summary	151

Introduction

An Overview of the Scriptures, by
BOB EVELY © *2018.*
An Independent Minister of Christ Jesus
Of the church at Wilmore, Kentucky

You knew not the era of your visitation (Luke 19:44).

The four gospels document the Lord's visitation upon the earth. Each writer had a specific purpose; these are not simply duplicate accounts from four different authors. We can discern the singular purpose from the focus and emphases of each account.

But before we begin our overview of the four gospels it will be important to consider a few things.

Is the Bible God's Word?

The things of God cannot be proven like a mathematical equation. Does God exist? Is the Bible really a revelation from God? Is the Koran a revelation of God? These things cannot really be proven or disproven scientifically. Instead we are presented with the evidence, much as a jury is expected to consider evidence as it works toward reaching a verdict.

There are many evidences that God exists. The creation all around us presents evidence of an intelligent, wise, creative and powerful Creator. The magic of life and the wonder of the human body are also evidence.

We are presented with various writings that scholars and others tell us are holy scriptures; revelations from God. Some tell us the Koran is God's revelation. Others say it is the Bible. Some make other claims. Do we base our verdict on the culture in which we live? Those raised in Islamic countries generally reach the verdict that the Koran is the Word of God. Those raised in Christian cultures commonly reach the verdict that the Bible is the Word of God. Some reach no verdict at all, believing that one cannot possibly know for sure. And some believe the verdict has no bearing on their life. But for those willing to examine the evidence, an <u>informed verdict</u> can be reached.

I believe the Bible is the Word of God, His revelation to mankind, because of the evidence. If the Bible is truly God's Word, believers

Introduction

cannot shy away from proclaiming it at every opportunity. It is truth not just among believers; but for the entire world.

But why do believers disagree in their Biblical interpretation?

It is fair to say that most Christian believers will agree as to what the Bible *says*. But there is much disagreement as to what the Bible *means*. Hence we have church divisions, hundreds of denominations and multitudes of individual churches teaching significantly different things. Arguments abound in Christian circles. In short, there is <u>great confusion</u> as to how the Bible is interpreted today.

God has *revealed* truth to mankind in His Word, but mankind has *confused* and *distorted* that truth because of carelessness, laziness and blindly following the specific church leaders one has chosen to follow.

There are two primary problems that cause confusion in understanding that which God has revealed.

Problem #1: A failure to have a pattern of sound words

Have a pattern of sound words, which you hear from me (2 Timothy 1:13).

There are many different Bible translations used today by well-meaning believers, thinking them to be the pure Word of God. But most have been written to either "dumb-down" the Word to make it easier to read and understand, or for the financial gain of the translators or publishers. In either case much truth is lost when the precise words intended by God to be preserved have been altered at the whim of the translators. Even well-meaning translators stray from sound words when they insert their own pre-developed opinions and understandings into the Word, making it more of a commentary based on the traditions and teachings of men than the pure Word of God.

Beware the traditions of the Pharisees (Matthew 15; Mark 7). While directed to the Jewish leaders of Jesus' day, this directive seems to have application with the church leaders of our day. As was the case in Jesus' day, religious leaders have inserted the traditions of men into Bible teachings. And like the average person in the Pharisees' day, churches today are filled with blind followers. Beware!

To truly understand that which God has chosen to reveal we must seek to study the Bible in as pure a form as possible. The original Hebrew and Greek manuscripts are no longer available to us, but we must use a translation that is faithful and accurate in our studies, using concordances that are based on the original languages.

Introduction

After having used many different Bible versions in my life, I now use primarily the Concordant Literal New Testament and the Concordant Version of the Old Testament, both published by the Concordant Publishing Concern. This is a literal translation and it was developed using consistent, logical principles ... *a pattern of sound words*. If God used two different Greek words in the originals the distinction is preserved, instead of combining several different Greek words into a single English word. God must have had reason to use different words, and we must strive to understand the distinctions if we are to accurately understand that which God has revealed.

Likewise if God used the same Greek word in different instances, the same idea (and even the same word when possible) is presented in the English.

Meanings of words are derived by using a concordance (hence the "Concordant" version) to examine every instance where a word is used in Scripture. And my favorite thing about this translation is the *Keyword Concordance* which is included. This allows the reader to take any English word used in the translation, identify the Greek word it came from, and look at every other instance where that same Greek word was used. This allows the reader to examine every word in all of its occurrences to see if the English word used in the translation is correct.

The Concordant Version can be ordered from *The Concordant Publishing Concern* at www.concordant.org

Another study help is *Young's Analytical Concordance*. Unlike the more commonly known *Strong's Concordance,* Young's is organized by the original Greek or Hebrew word that was used, enabling the reader to trace word usage and meaning in the original languages, even without training in Greek or Hebrew.

Problem #2: A failure to "rightly divide"

Endeavor to present yourself to God qualified, an unashamed worker, correctly cutting the word of truth (2 Timothy 2:15). In most translations *correctly cut* is translated *rightly divide*.

We must pay close attention to the context. To whom is God writing? Does the passage pertain directly to us in this present era, or was God working differently in that previous era, and perhaps with a different people group?

It is certainly true that *all scripture is inspired by God and is beneficial for teaching, for exposure, for correction, for discipline in righteousness,*

Introduction

that the man of God may be equipped, fitted out for every good act (2 Timothy 3:16). But this does not mean that all scripture is speaking directly *to* us in our present-day context. For example, if God speaks to those of Israel in a past era and context; we cannot *force* that passage to apply to our present situation. God is always the same God, but by His choice and to fulfill His purposes He has chosen to work differently in different eras.

Rightly dividing God's Word is a divine precept on the same level as all other of God's instructions. If we fail to rightly divide, confusion will reign and it will not be possible to understand that which God has revealed.

For example, when we read; *Go not into the way of the Gentiles ... but go rather to the lost sheep of Israel* (Matthew 10:5-6); we might think this to be in conflict with other passages that command disciples to *go into all the world*. But both are words of God and both must be true. We cannot simply discard one and retain the other, and we cannot allow one truth to upset another truth. The only solution is to "rightly divide" the word of God. One passage announces God's plan in one era, and the other shows how God is working at a later time.

Consider the common disagreements among believers, all of whom derive their understandings from the same Bible.

- ✓ Some believe the kingdom Jesus talks about is *heaven*. Others believe the kingdom is different from heaven and will actually come upon the *earth* when Jesus returns.
- ✓ Some believe when Jesus speaks to *Israel* we can apply His words directly to the *church* of our day, thinking the church has replaced Israel. Others believe it is important to distinguish between things spoken to Israel and things spoken to the church.
- ✓ People have many differing views of "the unpardonable sin" as found in Matthew 12.
- ✓ People have differing views as to what happens when we die. Do we go immediately to heaven or hell? Do we go into a sleep state awaiting the resurrection?
- ✓ People have differing views as to what will happen on the earth, and the order of events, in the end times. Some believe the end time events have already taken place.
- ✓ Some believe we have *free will* while others believe God has *determined* the course of events.

Again, most will agree as to what the Bible *says*. But opinions differ as to what the Bible *means*, or how it is to be interpreted. The problem within Christian circles today is the same as with the Pharisees of

Introduction

Jesus' day. The Word of God has been *transgressed* and *invalidated* by the traditions of men (Matthew 15:1-9). The Reformation recovered some truth that had been lost, but within several generations the church relapsed and allowed creeds and confessions to replace the Bible.

How do the various parts of the Bible fit together?

Many folks will memorize large portions of the Scriptures. While this is beneficial to a point, let me suggest that it is *far* more important to understand how all of the pieces of the Bible fit together. It is a mistake, leading to error and confusion, if one reaches into the Scriptures and arbitrarily applies any passage to their present situation. Memorization or instant recall of the Scriptures means *nothing* if one fails to understand how all of the various portions of Scripture fit into God's overall workings. As is so well expressed in the preface to the 16th century translation of the Bible by Miles Coverdale: "It shall greatly help ye to understand Scripture if thou mark not only what is spoken or written but: -- to whom, and by whom; with what words, and at what time; where, and to what intent; with what circumstance; considering what goeth before and what followeth." In short ...

> *"All Scripture is inspired by God, and is beneficial for teaching"* (2 Timothy 3:16)
>
> – BUT –
>
> *"Endeavor to present yourself to God qualified, an unashamed worker, correctly cutting the word of truth"* (2 Timothy 2:15).

The New Testament

With the principle of *rightly dividing* in mind, it would seem that the New Testament can be divided into four distinct parts.

The Visitation consists of the four gospel accounts that document the Lord's life and ministry upon the earth.

The Waiting (or "The Fellowship of Jewish Believers") consists of the first part of Acts and the letters written by the Jewish apostles and leaders to the ecclesia which then consisted exclusively of believers *among Israel*. These believers are encouraged to persevere and endure as they face persecution and trial, and as they await the return of their king to reign upon the earth in the restored kingdom.

The Pause (or "The Fellowship of All Believers") consists of Paul's ministry ... the second portion of Acts as Paul is commissioned as a 13th apostle and as he receives new revelation from God and a new

Introduction

commission ... and Paul's letters that contain this new revelation. This is especially true of his later letters. We will see a distinction even within Paul's letters, with his early ministry directed to Israel first and only to the nations when he is cast out of the synagogues in various locations ... and his later ministry that announces *secrets* concealed by God in times past and now revealed; and with the nations of equal stature with Israel. Here we see a pause in God's workings with Israel, His chosen people. Paul's writings are parenthetical proclamations during the pause. Israel is temporarily set aside to the benefit of the nations (Romans 11:25). Paul introduces new things that had been a *secret* (by God's choosing) in times past. For the first time God reveals thru Paul the Body of Christ; *called-out-ones* not just from among Israel but from among all nations. Those of the nations are joint heirs with no preference given to those of Israel, which had been the case in the past. The Body of Christ does not await Christ's return to reign upon the earth. Instead the expectation is for Christ to call the Body into the heavenly realm (1 Thessalonians 4:13ff).

The Return of the King. The book of Revelation records the events leading up to and culminating with the return of the king to reign in the restored kingdom upon the earth.

Think for yourself!

Most who study the Bible will agree that Jesus was physically resurrected, that believers will likewise be resurrected in the life to come, and that salvation comes through Jesus Christ. This is our common ground. Errors in translations and interpretations of the Bible have not clouded these major points. This is the foundation of our faith! It is this basic faith that differentiates the believer from the non-believer. But on many other points we differ in our understanding.

Many hold to their beliefs based upon their upbringing, their culture, the teachings of their pastor or professor, or the official doctrines of "The Church" (creeds, statements of faith, "orthodoxy"). But even these "experts" disagree on many specific points, and they cannot all be right.

I challenge you to consider the evidence and to think for yourself as you study the Bible! Theologies are nothing more than theories to be challenged and tested to be sure they are correct. Don't simply accept the theology that has been handed to you by your church or your pastor. Test it! Study and think for yourself.

If you think that your church, pastor or Bible teachers are correct in their understandings and teachings, consider this. Near the end of Paul's life nearly all had abandoned him and his teachings, and had

Introduction

turned away from truth. Near the end of Peter's life the same was true. At what point in history after their deaths do we think that church leaders and the majority opinions of the church got it right? I contend that the church remains in apostasy, and church leaders are being used by the Deceiver to cloud and distort the truth, and this is evidenced by the many different churches teaching significantly different things.

I have in my library a number of books and Bible commentaries, and on many points they disagree. No author, teacher or professor should be considered infallible and the final word. The fact that they disagree should show us that some, and perhaps all, are wrong in some matters.

I am simply asking you to study and to think for yourself. The overviews I have prepared on the New Testament writings represent my own perspectives. I don't claim to be right on all specifics and that everyone holding other views is wrong. I study the evidence and I think, and contained herein are my *theories* to be considered and tested.

You have been taught what the Bible means, and this has become the *theory* you now hold to be true. Challenge that theory. Examine the facts and evidences, and consider that your theory (and that of your "experts") might be wrong on some points. Open your Bible and study anew. Think for yourself!

Setting the stage for Matthew's account

As we prepare to start our New Testament overview, consider the events that unfolded throughout the Old Testament that set the stage for Matthew's account. God had established a kingdom upon the earth for His chosen people, the Israelites. As king of Israel, David brought unity and power to this kingdom. He was followed by Solomon, under whose reign the kingdom increased its borders and lived in peace. But after Solomon the kingdom declined sharply. Eventually both the northern portion of the kingdom (Israel) and the southern portion (Judah) were conquered, and the people were led away into exile. But there remained a light! Through the prophets God assured the people they would one day be returned to the land; and in fact they were. The temple was rebuilt, as were the walls of Jerusalem. As Matthew opens the people are back in their land, but it is not *their* land and they are not in control. The Roman government rules over Israel and it has been 400 years since the last of the prophets had spoken. The people await a further word from their God.

So in accord with Old Testament prophecies, Israel is waiting and watching for the restoration of the kingdom. They await their king; the

Introduction

Messiah. It is with this anticipation that Matthew begins. Let us begin our study, paying close attention to the details so as to clearly understand that which God has revealed.

Matthew

An Overview of the Scriptures, by
BOB EVELY © *2018.*
An Independent Minister of Christ Jesus
Of the church at Wilmore, Kentucky

CHAPTER 1

The lineage (1:1)

Matthew begins his account with a detailed lineage. Why? Could it be that his singular purpose in writing is to build a case concerning the qualifications of Jesus to be the Christ (the *Anointed One*)?

In fact, Matthew clearly documents that Jesus meets the prophetic requirements to be the Messiah, having descended from the line of Judah and David. Matthew reveals Jesus as the MESSIAH and the KING of Israel. The genealogy proves His title to the throne.

Special mention is made that Jesus is the *Son of David*. This would qualify him to be the successor to David's throne; the King who will reign when the kingdom is restored. And we are told he is the *Son of Abraham*, which would qualify Jesus to inherit the promises made to Abraham (the seed and the land).

> In Appendix 99 of the *Companion Bible*, Mr. Bullinger notes that there are several omissions from the genealogy. Between Joram and Ozias we would expect to see Ahaziah, Joash and Amaziah, and between Josias and Jechonias we would expect to see Jehoiakim and Jachoniah. But in both cases Mr. Bullinger points out that these omissions are due to their being blotted out in accord with the Law. (Deuteronomy 29:20) In the same Appendix 99, Mr. Bullinger displays the difference between the genealogies of Matthew and Luke. Matthew's genealogy presents the line from Abraham to Joseph, the earthly father of Jesus. Luke presents the line from Adam to Mary, the mother of Jesus. In the Luke account, Joseph is said to be the son of Heli, (Luke 3:23) although this is true only in the legal sense due to his marriage to Mary. According to the flesh Joseph is the son of Jacob.

The birth of Jesus is foretold (1:18)

When Mary is found to be with child, a messenger of the Lord tells Joseph that the child being generated in her is *of holy spirit*.

> While the genealogy documents that Jesus is the son of David and meets the requirements for being the Messiah and the inheritor of David's throne, His being generated of the holy spirit displays that He is also the *son of God.* He has a human element and a divine element.

The messenger tells Joseph the child is *to be named Jesus, for He shall be saving* HIS PEOPLE *from their sins.*

> As parents we often choose names for our children arbitrarily, but when God chooses a name it has meaning, and the meaning is often revealed to us in His Word. In this case we see that the name Jesus is associated with salvation. This, then, will tell us something of Jesus' purpose. Note also that Jesus' commission is announced ... to save HIS PEOPLE from their sins; ISRAEL.

The birth will fulfill what the prophet had declared, *The virgin shall be pregnant and shall be bringing forth a Son, and they shall be calling His name Emmanuel.* (Isaiah 7:14) This prophecy is being construed, *God with us.*

> Since Jesus has a divine nature, having been fathered by the holy spirit, He is the *son of God* and we could therefore say He is *God with us.* We will see throughout Matthew many references to the fulfillment of Old Testament prophecies. REMEMBER THAT THE PROPHETS SPOKE TO ISRAEL AND TO JUDAH, NOT TO THE ENTIRE WORLD.

CHAPTER 2

The birth of Jesus (2:1)

Jesus is born and magi from the East (Gentiles) come to worship this *King of the Jews.* Herod becomes disturbed over this and seeks to kill Jesus, causing Joseph and Mary to flee to Egypt.

> It is interesting that Gentiles recognize He is the King of the Jews, and yet the Jews do not.

Jesus' birth in Bethlehem fulfills another prophecy (Micah 5:2), a Messianic requirement that is recognized by the chief priests and scribes.

When Herod learns that the magi are not returning to tell him where to find the child, he is furious and kills all the boys in Bethlehem under two years of age. This fulfills yet another prophecy. (Jeremiah 31:15) When Herod dies a messenger of the Lord appears to Joseph in a trance, telling him to go to Israel. Another messenger later redirects him to Nazareth in Galilee.

Overview of MATTHEW

CHAPTER 3

John the Baptist (3:1)

In those days John the Baptist was proclaiming: *Repent! For near is the kingdom of the heavens.* Isaiah had prophesied John's heralding (Isaiah 40:3). Many come to John, confessing their sins, and are baptized by him. But when the Pharisees and Sadducees come, John proclaims: *Progeny of vipers! Who intimates to you to be fleeing from the impending indignation? Produce, then, fruit worthy of repentance.*

> Observe from John's words:
>> The kingdom of the heavens is *near*
>> There is coming an *indignation*
>> True repentance, manifested by *fruit*, is called for

WHAT IS THIS KINGDOM THAT JOHN IS PROCLAIMING? IS IT "HEAVEN?" IS IT SOMETHING THAT IS TO BE SOLELY "WITHIN" THOSE WHO BELIEVE?

Consider that David's kingdom was ordained by God and established upon the earth. Later the prophets proclaimed that there would be a restoration of this kingdom unto Israel with a successor king from David's lineage. Daniel foretold that this would be greater than all other kingdoms.

Many today believe that Matthew's references to the kingdom are not foretelling a return of the *physical* kingdom upon the earth, but are instead *figurative* references. But certainly the disciples were expecting a physical kingdom to come upon the earth after the resurrection (Acts 1:6) and Jesus does not tell them they have misunderstood. He simply tells them it is not theirs to know the timing of things that will take place. In Revelation we see Christ's return to the earth and the establishment of the kingdom in the eon that follows this present eon. Even in Revelation (21:1) in the final eon; when John perceives *a new heaven and a new earth* and sees *the holy city, new Jerusalem, descending out of heaven;* we note that the city <u>descends out of heaven</u>. The city is not heaven itself!

Throughout Revelation as the kingdom becomes a reality, there is a distinct Jewish character. The twelve tribes (21:12) and twelve apostles (21:14) are prominent. The nations are not found within the city but are outside. (21:24) How different this is from Paul's description of the heavenly realm with no barrier between Jew and Gentile. In Revelation the leaves on the tree are *for the cure of the nations*, (22:2) implying a physical body in need of the leaves to sustain life. Compare this with the incorruptible spiritual body described by Paul (1 Corinthians 15:42). When we hear of the lake of fire burning (Revelation 21:8) it is further described as the *second death*. But Paul tells us *the last enemy is being abolished: death*. (1 Corinthians 15:27) When we see Christ reigning upon the throne (Revelation 21:5) as promised by the prophets of old, we think of Paul's words; that Christ must reign UNTIL He places all enemies under His feet, and then when all is subject to Christ He subjects Himself to God, Who becomes All in all. (1 Corinthians 15:25,28) And when we hear that the slaves of God are reigning (Revelation 22:5) and that there are *kings of the earth*, (Revelation 21:24) we think of Paul's proclamation that all sovereignty, authority and power are nullified. (1 Corinthians 15:24)

Revelation describes the kingdom of heaven coming upon the earth with Christ reigning. This is the kingdom John the Baptist and Jesus announce in Matthew. But the king, and therefore the kingdom, are rejected by the Jews. During this time in which we now live, while Israel is temporarily set aside, salvation is given to the nations/Gentiles. (Romans 11:25) When God is ready the kingdom will come upon the earth, although it is not ours to know the timing. (Acts 1:7) And when God is ready, when at last every knee is bowing and all are subjected to Him, the final eon will come to its conclusion. (1 Corinthians 15) Death (the lake of fire) will be abolished, all will have found salvation through the grace of God and the work of Christ upon the cross, and God will be All in all.

Don't take my word for these things. Study the Scriptures diligently and question those things commonly taught by the organized church.

WHAT IS THE "IMPENDING INDIGNATION" THAT JOHN SPEAKS OF? IS IT "ETERNAL TORMENT?"

Those not producing ideal fruit will be cast into the fire. (3:10) As the kingdom comes upon the earth, judgment is coming. To be saved from this *indignation* one must have good works; "ideal fruit".

Consider John's message: Repent; the kingdom is near; indignation is coming. We will see in Paul's writings that this is not our message to proclaim in the present era, although many misguided churches are proclaiming John's message thinking it still pertains. More on this later when we look at Paul's letters. For now, let us simply pay close attention to whom the words in Matthew's account are directed; *Israel*.

Overview of MATTHEW

John announces One who is to come after him, who will not be baptizing in water but instead in holy spirit and fire. When Jesus comes He is baptized by John *to fulfill all righteousness*.

> Water baptism would not have been necessary for Jesus but He subjects Himself to it nonetheless to fulfill all righteousness; that for the sake of His "spectators" all conditions of Judaism are met. John also mentions a different type of baptism that Jesus will introduce at some point; a baptism *in holy spirit and fire* that appears to be intended to replace water baptism when introduced.

Immediately upon coming up from the water, the heavens open and He perceives the spirit of God descending as if a dove, and coming on Him. A voice out of heaven declares, This is My Son.

> The voice from heaven has confirmed that Jesus is the *Son of God*.

CHAPTER 4

The temptation of Jesus (4:1)

Jesus is led up into the wilderness by the spirit to be tried by the Adversary.

> Do we see here a parallel to Adam's being "led" by God into the Garden of Eden where he was tried by the serpent? The difference is that Adam disobeyed, resulting in death for all mankind. Jesus obeys and remains faithful to God, which will result in life for all mankind. *As it was through one offense for all mankind for condemnation, thus also it is through one just award for all mankind for life's justifying.* (Romans 5:18)

Jesus proclaims the evangel of the kingdom (4:17)

Jesus begins His ministry, and His message is the same as John's. *Repent! For near is the kingdom of the heavens.*

> Jesus is the king; heir to the throne of David. But the kingdom of heaven is not yet here; it is *near*.

Jesus calls four of His disciples; Peter, Andrew, James and John. He leads them through all of Galilee, TEACHING in the synagogues, HERALDING *the evangel of the kingdom*, and CURING every disease and debility.

> Observe that the message being proclaimed by Jesus ... *Repent! For near is the kingdom of the heavens* ... is referred to as *the evangel of the kingdom*.

> If we study the Greek word EVANGEL every time it occurs in the Scriptures we will see that it simply means *good news*. The word is translated *gospel* in most Bible translations. But when we think of "the gospel" our ideas have been biased by the system of theology we have been taught. In fact, the word EVANGEL SIMPLY MEANS GOOD NEWS; period! It is not always the same good news. Each time we encounter the word *evangel* we must ask ourselves, what is the good news being referred to in this passage? The Concordant Version simply uses the transliteration *evangel* instead of the word *gospel* so that our thinking will not be biased by any preconceived notions. In Matthew we see it is *the evangel of the kingdom* that is being proclaimed. If we study carefully we will note that this evangel is much different from what Paul will later proclaim to the Gentiles, who have their expectation in *the celestial kingdom* and not in the kingdom to come upon the earth.

Vast throngs follow Jesus, bringing to Him all who have illnesses and torments.

> There is a strong relationship between teaching, heralding and healing. But as we observe God's works in a particular era we cannot assume He will work in the same way in all eras. All we know from this account in Matthew is that there is a relationship between teaching, heralding and healing during this time when Jesus is proclaiming the evangel of the kingdom to Israel. This message pertains only to ISRAEL. When Paul is later commissioned to proclaim a different evangel to a different people group, we will see the decline of visible signs. Today the Body of Christ has its expectation in the celestial realm, not in this earthly realm. We have no expectation of a physical land. We await the Lord to snatch us away into the heavens, (1 Thessalonians 4:13ff) not to come and establish the kingdom here upon the earth. That is Israel's expectation, and it makes sense that a message concerning things to occur upon the earth would be accompanied by signs such as healing that have an effect in life upon the earth. This is not to say that God will no longer bring supernatural healing in some instances. I am simply suggesting that the connection we see in Matthew between teaching, heralding and healing no longer seems to be pertinent as we proclaim a different evangel; the evangel of peace, reconciliation, and grace that has been charged to us in this present era.

CHAPTER 5

Overview of MATTHEW

The "Beatitudes" (5:1)

Jesus announces that rewards are to come in the kingdom for certain individuals; those who are poor, who mourn, who are meek, who are hungering for righteousness, who are merciful, who are clean in heart, who are peacemakers and who are persecuted. The rewards will be consolation, an allotment of the land, satisfaction, mercy, the ability to see God, the right to be called sons of God and vast wages.

> Some of these rewards, especially an *allotment of the land*, show us that the expectation at that time is the kingdom to come upon the earth, and not "heaven." We have no right to *spiritualize* these words of Jesus, causing the *kingdom* to become *heaven*. It is real land upon the earth that is to be enjoyed by Israel when the kingdom is restored.

Rules for the Kingdom (5:13)

The following topics are addressed by Jesus in what is commonly called the "sermon on the mount."
- ✓ They are to be salt and light
- ✓ Jesus came to fulfill the law
- ✓ *Superabounding righteousness* is required to enter the kingdom (5:20)
- ✓ Not only murder is prohibited, but also anger
- ✓ One must reconcile with his brother before bringing offerings
- ✓ One should settle before going to the judge
- ✓ Not only adultery is prohibited, but also lust
- ✓ No divorce
- ✓ No oaths
- ✓ Turn the other cheek
- ✓ Love your enemy
- ✓ *Be perfect* as your heavenly Father is perfect (5:48)

> CERTAINLY THESE WORDS CAN CONVEY CERTAIN PRINCIPLES FOR US TODAY, BUT WE MUST BE VERY CAREFUL AS TO HOW WE APPLY THEM. Remember that Jesus is speaking to the Jews of His day, getting them ready to live within the kingdom when it is restored upon the earth. We cannot assume that things stated to the Jews of this particular era will automatically apply to non-Jews in the 21st century.
>
> Is GEHENNA really "hell" as most Bible translations would have us believe?
>
> The Greek word *gehenna*, translated *hell* in most English translations, is first mentioned in Matthew 5:22. It is the Greek form of the Hebrew *Gai Hinnom* or *Valley of Hinnom*. This is a physical place; a ravine just below Jerusalem. This place is referred to in 2 Chronicles 28:3 and 33:6.

In Jesus' day it was a refuse dump with fires perpetually burning. When Jesus talked about *Gehenna* his audience understood that He referred to this refuse dump outside of Jerusalem. For certain crimes once the kingdom is restored, the bodies of the guilty will be cast into this place; a disgraceful fate. Isaiah 66:22-24 foretells this, and the terminology used shows that it is clearly a physical and not a spiritual location. *All flesh* will see the corpses of the *mortals* burning in the fire as they come to Jerusalem to worship.

This was Jesus' first reference to *Gehenna*. Had He been referring to a spiritual place of endless torment, something different from the *Valley of Hinnom* that the Jews were familiar with, this would have been a new concept and many questions would have been asked and clarifications needed. From Genesis forward the penalty for sin is death, not endless torment. If Jesus is changing the penalty to endless torment, surely He would have provided further explanation as to this change.

CHAPTER 6

- ✓ Do your righteousness in private
- ✓ Pray in private
- ✓ No useless repetitions when praying
- ✓ The "Lord's Prayer"
- ✓ Forgive others
- ✓ When fasting, do it secretly
- ✓ Hoard treasures in heaven, not on earth
- ✓ The eye is the lamp of the body
- ✓ One cannot serve two lords; God and mammon
- ✓ Do not worry; seek first the kingdom

The words of the "LORD'S PRAYER" (6:9) are clearly speaking of a kingdom to come upon the earth, *as it is in heaven*. Those of Israel that Jesus is addressing do not have an expectation of "going to heaven," but instead that the kingdom will come upon the earth. While this prayer is repeated weekly in many of today's churches, it is really a prayer intended for Jewish believers in Jesus' day. The expectation of the Body of Christ is to be called upward to be with the Lord and to serve Him there, in the celestial realms.

CHAPTER 7

- ✓ Do not judge
- ✓ Don't give what is holy to curs
- ✓ Ask, seek, knock
- ✓ Do to others what you would have done to you
- ✓ Narrow is the gate leading to life

- ✓ Beware of false prophets
- ✓ Not all saying *Lord* will enter the kingdom; but only those <u>doing</u> the Father's will

> Now consider these RULES FOR LIVING IN THE KINGDOM OF HEAVEN that is to come upon the earth. Lewis Sperry Chafer observes in his "Systematic Theology," *It will be found that the teachings of the kingdom represented in the Sermon on the Mount are in exact accord with the Old Testament predictions regarding the kingdom, and are almost wholly in disagreement with the teachings of grace.*
>
> Yes, these words may contain some principles for today since they express the heart of God relative to certain human behaviors. But they will be strictly enforced rules for those living in the kingdom when it comes upon the earth, which we will see fulfilled in Revelation when Christ returns to reign.
>
> What are the conditions for entering the kingdom when it is restored upon the earth? SUPERABOUNDING RIGHTEOUSNESS (5:20) and PERFECTION. (5:48) Observe that the evangel of the kingdom is WORKS-ORIENTED. And note that for certain crimes death will be the punishment, with the body of the guilty party cast into Gehenna.

The throngs are astonished, for Jesus taught as One having authority, unlike the scribes.

CHAPTER 8

Miracles accompany the evangel (8:1)
- ✓ A leper is healed (8:1)
- ✓ A centurion's son is healed (8:5)
- ✓ Peter's mother-in-law is healed (8:14)
- ✓ Many are healed and demons cast out (8:16)

Vast throngs follow (8:18)

A disciple asks for time to bury his father before following. Jesus replies, Follow Me and leave the dead to entomb their own dead.

> His message to the disciples: Set aside worldly entanglements and focus on the things of God.

Miracles accompany the evangel (8:23)
- ✓ The sea is calmed (8:23)
- ✓ Two demoniacs are healed (8:28)

CHAPTER 9

- ✓ A paralytic is healed (9:1)
- ✓ A dead girl is raised (9:18)
- ✓ A woman with bleeding is healed (9:20)
- ✓ Two blind men are healed (9:27)
- ✓ Demons are cast out of a mute demoniac (9:33)

> We previously observed the close relationship between proclaiming the kingdom evangel and miracles. (4:23) It seems that miracles were one of the *means* used to proclaim the kingdom.
>
> ARE MIRACLES TO BE EXPECTED IN OUR PRESENT DAY? Healings and other miracles were prevalent in these days as the kingdom evangel is being proclaimed. But we state once again, this does not necessarily mean that miracles will continue to be the norm in later eras, as when Paul later proclaims the evangel entrusted to him. This is not to say that God could not perform miracles even in our present day; most certainly He can. But could it be that miracles served a purpose in proclaiming the kingdom evangel which was focused on earthly blessings for Israel, that is perhaps not served in Paul's message that *grace is sufficient*. We will think about this more when we study Paul's letters, but for now let us keep this possibility in mind as we continue our study of Matthew.

Criticism (9:3)

Some of the scribes criticize Jesus for pardoning the sins of the paralytic. Matthew is called to follow and becomes a disciple. Jesus is criticized for eating with sinners. He replies that He came not to call the just, but sinners. John's disciples ask Jesus why His disciples do not fast. Jesus replies that they will fast when the bridegroom is taken away.

> They have no reason to fast now as the bridegroom is with them. Fasting seems to be linked with a longing or a desire for the bridegroom to come.
>
> Jesus observes the cause of their criticism; they are putting fresh wine into old wine skins. (9:17) Jesus is bringing new teachings and they are not fitting into the old understandings.

Miracles and criticism (9:18)

- ✓ Jesus raises a girl that had died
- ✓ He heals a woman that had a hemorrhage for twelve years
- ✓ Two blind men are healed
- ✓ A mute demoniac is healed

The Pharisees criticize Jesus, saying that the healings were done *by the chief of demons*.

Overview of MATTHEW

Teaching, heralding, healing (9:35)

Jesus goes about all the cities and villages, TEACHING in the synagogues, HERALDING the evangel of the kingdom, and CURING every disease and debility.

> Again we see the strong connection between His heralding the kingdom evangel and healing.

He has compassion for the throngs, noting they are as sheep without a shepherd and that the harvest is great but the workers are few.

CHAPTER 10

Commissioning the Twelve (10:1)

Jesus calls His twelve disciples and gives them authority to heal the infirm, to rouse the dead, to cleanse the lepers and to cast out demons. They are to go ONLY TO THE LOST SHEEP OF ISRAEL (10:6) and are to herald the message, *Near is the kingdom of the heavens.*

Only to ISRAEL!

> Observe very closely ... Jesus commissioned ONLY the Twelve, and they were to go ONLY TO THE LOST SHEEP OF ISRAEL and not to the Gentiles. To ignore the context provided in the Scriptures and to apply things to ourselves that were given to Israel is STEALING. And doing so causes us to misunderstand the revelation God has provided to us in His Word.
>
> We cannot claim, at least not from this passage, that our commission is the same today. This commission was given to a specific group of people at a specific time and for a specific purpose.
>
> Note: The words *commission* and *apostle* are both from the same Greek word *apostello*. An apostle is one who has been *commissioned*.

Jesus further instructs the Twelve. If they are not received, they are to move on. They will face persecution, and when they are led before governors and kings this will allow them to be a testimony to the nations.

Overview of MATTHEW

> A side-benefit of their heralding to Israel would be a *testimony to the nations*. But they are not commissioned to go to the nations; only to Israel.

When persecuted, they are to flee to another city. They are not to fear those killing the body alone, but Him Who is able to destroy the soul as well as the body in Gehenna.

> What is the difference between killing the body and killing the soul? They were not to fear the one able to kill the body only, but the One able to kill both body and soul. (10:28) A study of the Greek words used will reveal that the *soul* is generated when the body (from the soil) and spirit (from God) are joined. At death the body returns to the soil, the spirit returns to God, and the soul goes to *hades* (literally *the unseen*). This is true for all men, including both the righteous and the wicked. At the resurrection the soul lives again. This will occur in the next eon, when those in Christ will enjoy eonian life. But those not in Christ will remain in the unseen place. One need not fear a man who can kill only the body, for the soul will re-appear in the next eon at the resurrection. (1 Thessalonians 4:13ff) Instead one should fear God, Who is able to destroy the body *and* keep the soul in hades, thereby forfeiting life in the eon to come. Despite this, however, God will ultimately restore all mankind once the eons have concluded. (1 Corinthians 15)

They are to take care not to disown Jesus before men, or they too will be disowned before the Father. They are not to mistakenly think that Jesus came to bring peace. He came to cast a sword.

> He came to divide those following Him from those disowning Him.

The one who prefers a family member to Jesus is not worthy of Him. To be worthy one must take his cross and follow. The one who receives the Twelve is receiving Jesus and the One Who commissioned Jesus.

> Here we see a clear distinction between Jesus, and the One who commissioned Him; God.

CHAPTER 11

Once Jesus had finished commissioning the Twelve, He continues with His own teaching and heralding.

John the Baptist (11:2)

John the Baptist sends his disciples to Jesus asking, Are You the One? Instead of a direct response, Jesus answers by pointing to the things taking place; the miracles and the evangel being proclaimed to the poor.

> This seems to imply that the purpose of these manifestations is to say, "I am the One." Since miracles accompany the teaching and preaching concerning the kingdom (4:23; 9:35) it would seem that the purpose of these miracles is to proclaim in a way more powerful than words that the kingdom is near. If this is true, and if Israel and the coming kingdom are temporarily set aside (Romans 11:25) what can we infer about miracles in our present day? Perhaps until God turns once again to Israel, this may not be the day for miracles.

When John's disciples leave, Jesus speaks of John to the throngs. John is more than a prophet; he is the one of whom Malachi spoke. (Malachi 4:5-6) There are none greater among those born of women, but he is still less than the smallest in the kingdom. He is Elijah who is about to be coming.

> If John is the greatest among men, yet lesser than any in the kingdom, how will it be possible for *any* to enter the kingdom when it comes upon the earth? Could it be that the "kingdom rules" (sermon on the mount) are requirements that cannot possibly be fully observed by any man? Could it be these requirements were given to show man his incapability of entering the kingdom thru self-righteousness and works, and that full dependence on Christ is needed? When Christ does return could it be that what we read in Revelation is describing a process for preparing man to enter the kingdom? Think about these things as we continue our study throughout the New Testament.

Jesus teaches concerning the kingdom (11:12)

From the days of John the Baptist the kingdom of the heavens is being snatched by the violent.

> We see this in the opposition of the Jewish leaders against John and Jesus as they proclaim the evangel of the kingdom.

As for the cities who witness His powerful deeds but do not repent, woe unto them. If these acts had been witnessed in Tyre and Sidon long ago, they WOULD HAVE REPENTED.

> BUT WHY WERE TYRE AND SIDON NOT GIVEN THE SAME OPPORTUNITY OF WITNESSING MIRACLES THAT MIGHT CAUSE THEM TO REPENT? If the unrepentant in Tyre and Sidon are cast into an endless torment, this would not seem just. But if ultimately every knee

> will bow and if all will be reconciled, then what appears to be an injustice against Tyre and Sidon may have actually served a purpose as God works progressively thru history toward the goal of reconciling all mankind unto Himself.

Likewise, it will be *more tolerable for Sodom* in the day of judging than for Capernaum. Capernaum will subside to *the unseen*.

> *Unseen* is the Greek word *hades* and is translated *hell* in the KJV and *depths* in the NIV. If the people of Sodom will receive a lesser judgment than Capernaum, what will their judgment be? If both experience endless torment as some would teach, how is one receiving a lesser judgment than the other?

Things are hidden from the wise and intelligent and revealed to minors. Likewise, *none are recognizing the Father except the Son and he to whom the Son should be intending to unveil Him*.

> In other words, the things of God cannot be "figured out" or *violently* secured by the intelligence of man. Man is dependent upon God revealing these things in the time and manner that He chooses.

CHAPTER 12

Lord of the Sabbath ^(12:1)

When Jesus' disciples pick grain on the Sabbath the Pharisees object, saying this is unlawful. But Jesus reminds them that when David hungered he violated the Sabbath law by eating the holy bread designated only for the priests. (1 Samuel 21:6) And on the sabbaths the priests in the sanctuary profane the sabbath but are faultless. But One greater than the sanctuary is here. If the accusers knew the meaning of, Mercy am I wanting and not sacrifice, (Hosea 6:6) they would not convict the faultless, for the Son of Man is Lord of the Sabbath.

Jesus proceeds to heal a man with a withered hand on the Sabbath and again the Pharisees object. Jesus replies, It is allowed to be doing ideally on the sabbaths.

> A strict legal observance of the sabbath law would prevent the doing of any work, but Jesus had authority to bring a new truth; a higher truth. His teachings (new wine) were not easily fitting into the strict observation of the law (old wineskins).

The Pharisees make plans to kill Jesus (12:14)

As Jesus leaves, many follow Him and He cures them all. And He tells them they should not be making Him manifest.

> Up to this time Jesus had openly proclaimed the kingdom, and He commissions the Twelve to do the same. Now He tells those being healed not to make Him manifest. So, WE SEE A CHANGE as to how the kingdom evangel is proclaimed. Once declared openly; it will now be done somewhat in secret.

The unpardoned sin (12:22)

Jesus heals a blind and mute demoniac, and the crowds appear to recognize that He is the Son of David. But the Pharisees quickly object, alleging that Jesus is casting out demons by Beezeboul, the chief of demons. Jesus points out that if Satan casts out Satan, he divides himself and his kingdom cannot stand. And if by God's spirit Jesus is casting out demons, then *the kingdom of God outstrips in time to you.*

> In other words, the kingdom was coming before they were ready. Before one can plunder the house of one who is strong, that one must first be bound. So the casting out of demons must take place before the kingdom of God can come, replacing the kingdom of Satan.

Therefore (so what follows is related to what has just been said), *every sin and blasphemy shall be pardoned men, yet the blasphemy of the spirit shall not be pardoned. And whoever may be saying a word against the Son of Mankind it will be pardoned him, yet whoever may be saying aught against the holy spirit it shall not be pardoned him, neither in this eon nor in that which is impending.*

> Much has been said, and many speculations made, concerning *the unpardoned sin* ("unpardonable" in some translations). From the entire context we see that the offenders were guilty not because they opposed Jesus, but because they attributed the work of God to Satan. God's holy spirit was operating, but they claimed it was the power of Satan. Such rejection of God, or failure to recognize God, will not be forgiven in the PRESENT EON nor in the IMPENDING EON.
>
> Eon (*aion* in the Greek) is often translated eternal, carrying the thought of endlessness. But observe here two different eons; the *present* eon and the *impending* eon. Eon must, therefore, be a finite period of time with beginning and end. There is the present eon and another eon yet to come in the future. And as for those committing *the unpardoned sin*, they will not be forgiven in this present eon or in the one to follow, but this

Overview of MATTHEW

> does not mean forgiveness will not come after that. The unpardoned sin does not condemn a person "forever and ever."

This wicked generation (12:33)

A tree is known by its fruit. By one's words will he be justified or convicted. A man will give account concerning every idle declaration in the day of judgment.

The Pharisees and scribes ask for a sign, but Jesus replies that no sign will be given beyond the sign of Jonah. As Jonah was in the whale for three days and nights, so also the Son of Man will be in the earth. The Ninevites repented at Jonah's heralding, but not so with *this wicked generation*. The queen of the south journeyed to hear Solomon's wisdom, but not so with this generation; and more than Solomon is here.

When an unclean spirit leaves a man and cannot find rest, it returns to its home. And finding the home unoccupied it will bring other spirits even more wicked to dwell there, making it even worse than before. Thus it will be to this wicked generation.

> This appears to be speaking of more than demon possession, in the context of the entire generation of Israel. Could it be speaking of Israel's religion? Idolatry had gone, but Israel was now empty. She had come out of captivity, but was not filled with the spirit.

Jesus' mother and brothers (12:46)

When Jesus is told His mother and brothers are waiting to speak with Him, He replies, Anyone whoever should be doing the will of My Father Who is in the heavens, he is My brother and sister and mother!

> Jesus is not telling His listeners to disown their familes. He is using exaggerated language to teach the truth that doing God's will is more important than any other responsibility.

CHAPTER 13

Parables (13:1)

Jesus tells the throngs many things in parables, beginning with the parable of the sower. He later explains this parable to His disciples. (13:18) It refers to the message concerning the kingdom. Some will not understand and the wicked one will snatch away what has been sown. Some will receive the word with joy, but when affliction comes they will be snared. Some will hear, but are distracted by the worry of this eon

Overview of MATTHEW

and there will be no fruit. But some hear and understand, and bear fruit.

The disciples ask Jesus why He speaks in parables to the throngs. He answers, *To you has it been given to know the SECRETS of the kingdom of the heavens, yet to those it has not been given.*

> Parables were not used to make truth easier to understand, but to reveal secrets to some while CONCEALING them from others.
>
> At first the kingdom was proclaimed openly, but the Jewish leaders began rejecting it. Now Jesus proclaims in parables to conceal from most while revealing only to His closest followers; those to whom He has chosen to reveal. Remember, *No one is recognizing the Son except the Father; neither is anyone recognizing the Father except the Son and he to whom the Son should be intending to unveil Him.* (11:27) The use of parables is one of the ways He accomplishes this. Those accepting the evangel of the kingdom are those to whom the Father is revealed, and those rejecting the kingdom are those to whom the Father is not being revealed. Jesus explains, *Therefore in parables am I speaking to them, seeing that, observing, they are not observing, and hearing, they are not hearing, neither are they understanding. And filled up in them is the prophecy of Isaiah, that is saying, 'In hearing, you will be hearing, and may by no means be understanding, and observing, you will be observing, and may by no means be perceiving.' For stoutened is the heart of this people.* (13:13; Isaiah 6:9,10)
>
> With these words it seems that **THE KINGDOM HAS BEEN "LOCKED"** to the majority, with explanations and revelation given only to the closest disciples. The quote from Isaiah shows the intent that the people will be hearing, but not understanding; for their hearts are *stoutened.* From this point on Jesus speaks to the throngs only in parables.
>
> Remember that Jesus began by proclaiming the kingdom was NEAR, but now it appears to be LOCKED for the remainder of His ministry. Jumping ahead for a moment, Jesus will later tell the Jewish leaders, *you are* locking *the kingdom of the heavens in front of men. For you are not entering, neither are you letting those entering to enter* (Matthew 23:13). Peter is given the keys; *I will be giving you the keys of the kingdom of the heavens,* (Matthew 16:19) and in Acts 2 we see Peter use the keys to "unlock" the kingdom, proclaiming it openly once again. But after repeated rejection, and especially after the the rejection by the Jewish leaders in the final chapter of Acts, the kingdom is locked once

Overview of MATTHEW

again. Paul uses the same words from Isaiah 6 that Jesus had used to lock the kingdom. And today the Jews, and the kingdom's coming upon the earth, are delayed *until the complement of the nations may be entering.* (Romans 11:25) Paul's *evangel of the uncircumcision* (Galatians 2:7) is now the appropriate message until it is time once again for the *kingdom evangel* to be proclaimed; which will happen during the Tribulation period recorded by John in Revelation. But for now let us continue our study of Matthew.

More parables (13:24)

Jesus proceeds to share more parables with the throngs, *and apart from a parable He spoke nothing to them.* To those understanding, Jesus teaches things concerning the kingdom that had previously been *hid.*

The weeds (13:24)	Let the weeds grow together with the good seed until the harvest time.
The mustard seed (13:31)	The kingdom starts small, and grows large.
The yeast (13:33)	A small amount leavens the entire batch.
The weeds explained (13:36)	At the end of the eon the weeds will be culled by messengers and burned. (Note that even the disciples did not understand the parable until it was explained.)
The hidden treasure (13:44)	The kingdom is like hidden treasure.
The pearl (13:45)	The kingdom is like a merchant seeking a pearl.
The net (13:47)	The kingdom is like a net gathering all varieties, and at the end of the eon the rotten will be cast out.
The scribe (13:52)	A scribe who is made a disciple in the kingdom is like a man who takes new and old things from his treasure.

Note the emphasis on works (not faith) in the truths concerning entering the kingdom. Those *doing lawlessness* will be culled out.

Miracles (13:53)

Jesus returns to His own country, but those knowing His family wonder how He could have wisdom or perform powerful deeds. They were *snared.* Jesus observes, A prophet is not dishonored except in his own country and in his home. And He does not do many powerful deeds there *because of their unbelief.*

It appears that MIRACLES follow BELIEF as the kingdom evangel is proclaimed, and where there is unbelief there will be no miracles. Miracles were a *means* used by Jesus during the time He proclaimed the nearness of the kingdom. They became less frequent as disbelief and rejection grew.

Ultimately the kingdom was rejected and the king was crucified. It cannot be assumed that miracles are still used by God today just because He used them in this previous context. We live in a different "administration" and God may choose to work in different ways than He did during the "kingdom administration." Today we do not proclaim the kingdom is *near*, we proclaim grace and reconciliation with God. (2 Corinthians 5:20) Miracles were used by God <u>to demonstrate the nearness of the earthly kingdom</u>. But are miracles still needed by God to demonstrate His grace and reconciliation to the world? Certainly God is the same in all ages, but He may choose to work differently from one age to the next to suit His purposes. We cannot put God in a box and assume He will always work in the same way in all ages and circumstances.

CHAPTER 14

Jesus learns of John the Baptist's death and retires into the wilderness, privately. He has compassion on the throngs and heals those who are ailing. He miraculously feeds 5000 who had followed Him into the wilderness. He walks on the water, displaying His authority over nature. And at Gennesaret all who have an illness are brought to Him, and those who touch the tassel of His cloak are healed,

CHAPTER 15

Error of the Pharisees: Tradition (15:1)

The scribes and Pharisees say the disciples are transgressing the *tradition* of the elders by not washing their hands before eating. Jesus responds that the scribes and Pharisees transgress *the precept of God*, and they *invalidate the word of God* because of their tradition.

> The religious leaders had placed their own traditions above the word of God itself.

- It is not what goes into a man's mouth that contaminates him, but what comes out. Things going into a man eventually come out. But things coming out of a man's mouth have originated from his heart, and this contaminates the man. Jesus cites some examples: wicked reasonings, murders, adulteries, prostitutions, thefts, false testimonies, calumnies.

> In other words it is a man's heart (his inner being) that makes him clean or unclean. What is within a man is manifested in the things coming out of him.

The disciples point out that the Pharisees are snared at Jesus' words. Jesus replies that every plant that is not planted by God will be uprooted. He describes the Pharisees as *blind guides* of the blind.

> Enforcement of legal requirements by the Jewish leaders attempted to regulate conduct based on *outward* traits. But Jesus is showing them it is the *inner* man that is considered by God, not the outward.

Healing a Gentile (15:21)

Jesus is approached by a Canaanite woman asking Him to heal her demonized daughter. Jesus points out that He was NOT COMMISSIONED EXCEPT FOR THE LOST SHEEP OF ISRAEL. (15:24) But the woman persists, worshipping Jesus. She reminds Jesus that even puppies eat the scraps falling from the master's table. Jesus replies, Great is your faith, and He heals the daughter.

> **Again we see that Jesus' commission is exclusively TO THE LOST SHEEP OF ISRAEL!**

Gentiles are only blessed indirectly, as in this case. Yet many Gentiles in the organized church today try to take all that Jesus said to Israel in the era of His earthly ministry and apply it directly to the church today. "*All Scripture is inspired by God, and is beneficial for teaching ...*" (2 Timothy 3:16) – BUT – "*Endeavor to present yourself to God qualified, an unashamed worker, correctly cutting* ["rightly dividing" in many translations] *the word of truth.*" (2 Timothy 2:15)

WHAT CAN WE LEARN FROM THE CANAANITE WOMAN ABOUT WORSHIP?

The Greek word translated <u>worship</u> is *proskuneo*, which literally means "toward-teem." Our notion of what worship consists of has been shaped by the religious traditions and ideas of men. To determine the true meaning of worship as used in the Scriptures we should examine every instance where the word is used. Using the Keyword Concordance which is contained within the Concordant Literal New Testament, we can study every occurrence of *proskuneo*.

Overview of MATTHEW

> We read that the Canaanite woman *coming, worships Him.* (15:6) We learn from this instance that worship does not always occur within a group setting, and it is not always done thru singing as some today believe. If we examine every occurrence of the word in the New Testament we will see that worship is simply a coming near, a reverence for, and a faith in the object of worship; whatever outward shape this may take. Let the reader search every occurrence of *proskuneo* to see what the Lord has revealed concerning worship.

Healings (15:30)

Vast throngs come to Jesus with their lame, blind, mute and maimed, and He cures them. The throngs marvel and glorify the God of ISRAEL. Jesus miraculously feeds 4000.

CHAPTER 16

Beware of the Pharisees (16:1)

Jesus refers to the generation as *wicked and an adulteress.* He tells the Pharisees and Sadducees that no sign will be given them except the sign of Jonah.

> Signs and wonders have been plentiful, but perhaps not in the presence of the Jewish leaders. Where there is unbelief, there will be no signs. (13:58)

Jesus warns His disciples to *take heed of the leaven of the Pharisees and Sadducees.* The disciples think Jesus is talking about literal bread and He tells them they are *scant of faith.* He explains that His reference was made to the *teaching* of the Pharisees and Sadducees.

> We must always take care as we study God's Word to determine whether it is making reference to something literal or if it is speaking figuratively, lest we misinterpret what the Scriptures are revealing.

Upon this rock will I build ... (16:13)

Jesus asks His disciples who men are saying the Son of Man is. Some are saying he is John the Baptist, or Elijah, or Jeremiah or one of the prophets. Jesus asks who they, the disciples, say that He is. Peter replies, Thou art the Christ, the Son of the living God. Immediately thereafter Jesus says to Peter, *You are Peter, and on this rock will I be building My ecclesia, and the gates of the unseen shall not be prevailing against it. I will be giving you the keys of the kingdom of the heavens.* (16:18-19)

On this rock could refer to Peter, or it could refer to Peter's *faith* that prompted his acknowledgement of Jesus being the Christ. The Greek word for Peter is *petros*, and the Greek for rock is *petra*.

DOES THIS PASSAGE REPRESENT THE BEGINNING OF "THE CHURCH?"

Most within the organized church today insist that this is the case as it is typically translated *upon this rock will I be building my church*. The Greek *ekklesia*, usually (though not always) translated *church*, simply means <u>called-out-ones</u> (*ek* - out; *klesia* - called). If we examine *ekklesia* in every instance where it is found we will see that it does not always refer to the same group of called-out-ones in every case. It is used to refer to an assembly in Moses' day, (Acts 7:38) an unruly mob, (Acts 19:32) and a legal assembly like a jury. (Acts 19:39) An ecclesia is simply a group of people *called out* from the general masses for a particular purpose. Even in cases where ecclesia is a group that God has *called out*, can we assume it is always the same group (i.e. today's church)? Those called out in Jesus' day and in the book of Acts were exclusively Jewish believers whose expectation was the kingdom from heaven to come upon the earth. But those called out in Paul's day are Jews and Gentiles alike called into one "body," whose expectation is in the heavenly realm. (1 Thessalonians 4:13) Therefore when Jesus proclaims to Peter, *On this rock will I build My ecclesia*, He speaks of the out-called Jews who are hearing the kingdom evangel and who are preparing for the kingdom to be established upon the earth, as it had been in David's day.

Are "the keys of the kingdom" related to the "locking" of the kingdom?

When Jesus says to Peter, *I will be giving you the KEYS of the kingdom of the heavens*, this implies that the kingdom is "locked" and that keys are needed to open it. This concept is confirmed by the fact that Jesus has been talking about the kingdom only thru parables to conceal understanding from the masses. When the holy spirit comes at Pentecost (Acts 2) we see the keys coming to Peter. Peter becomes the focal point and is given signs and wonders to accompany the kingdom proclamation, as had been the case when Jesus proclaimed the kingdom. But as the kingdom continues to be rejected by the Jews in Acts, Peter fades and Paul takes the forefront. The keys given to Peter are no longer in use as Acts comes to an end. A new age had begun. Paul no longer proclaims the kingdom evangel to the Jews but instead the evangel of grace and reconciliation to the Gentiles.

One last caution. We note that Jesus gives authority to Peter to bind on the earth those things that have been bound in the heavens and to loose on the earth those things that have been loosed in the heavens. Note that this authority is given to Peter and to no others. This statement relates to the kingdom of heaven coming upon the earth. Satan has no power in heaven, and there are none who are sick or demon possessed except upon the earth. Signs and wonders accompany Peter's proclamation of the kingdom evangel which relates to the kingdom to be restored upon the earth.

Jesus predicts His death (16:21)

Immediately after Peter's acknowledgement that Jesus is the Christ, and after talking about the building of His ecclesia, Jesus predicts His death. He must come to Jerusalem where He will suffer and be killed, and on the third day roused. Peter objects, This shall not be. Jesus replies, *Go away behind Me, satan! ... you are not disposed to that which is of God, but that which is of men.*

> The word *satan* in the Greek is a direct transliteration of the Hebrew word *satan*, and means *adversary*. In objecting to the words of Jesus, Peter is acting as an adversary to that which is of God.

The cost of following (16:24)

If any want to come after Me let him renounce himself and pick up his cross and follow Me. For whosoever may be wanting to save his soul shall be destroying it. Yet whoever should be destroying his soul on My account shall be finding it. For what will a man be benefited if he should be gaining the whole world yet forfeiting his soul?

> There is a cost to following Jesus. The disciple finds it necessary to renounce himself to follow. And if, when faced with the decision, one seeks to preserve his own life instead of following, he shall instead be destroying his life. Even if one gains *the whole world,* what would that matter if his soul is forfeited.

Overview of MATTHEW

> But if one gains the whole world, how is it that he loses his life (soul)? This is speaking of the contrast between this present life and the life to come after death. We see this in the words that follow. *For the Son of Mankind is about to be coming in the glory of His Father, with His messengers, and then He will be paying each in accord with his practice.* (16:27) If one did not persevere in life, where works are being evaluated, he would forfeit his place in the resurrection when the kingdom comes upon the earth. Remember this is speaking to the Jews who Jesus came to gather. All we have seen thus far in Jesus' words is <u>works oriented</u> and directed to Israel. The choice is to reject Jesus in preference of one's own life, thereby forfeiting life in the age to come ... or to follow Jesus even if this leads to death, thereby gaining life in the age to come. But take heart; even those forfeiting life in the age to come will ultimately be reconciled to God when He becomes All in all. (1 Corinthians 15)

CHAPTER 17

The "transfiguration" (17:1)

Jesus selects Peter, James and John to witness His *transformation* on the mountain. Moses and Elijah are seen talking with Jesus, and a voice from a cloud is heard to say, *This is My Son, the Beloved, in Whom I delight. Hear Him*! Jesus later tells the disciples not to tell anyone of the vision they had witnessed *till the Son of Mankind may be roused from among the dead.*

> So once again Jesus tells them of His death and resurrection.

The disciples ask why the scribes say that Elijah must come first. *Elijah is indeed coming, and will be restoring all. Yet I am saying to you that Elijah came already, and they did not recognize him.*

> They understood that Jesus was referring to John the Baptist. Certainly John is not the reincarnation of Elijah, for the Bible does not teach reincarnation. I take this to mean that Elijah was a "type" of what John the Baptist later came to be. We might say that John was of the spirit of Elijah. Elijah is not the person who will come and restore all, but he is a "type" of the One Who would do so.

Another healing (17:14)

Jesus heals an epileptic boy by casting a demon from him.

> We see a connection, at least in this case, between demon possession and illness. Jesus *heals* a boy having a *demon*.

Overview of MATTHEW

The disciples had previously tried to cast out this demon but were not successful, and Jesus tells them it was because of their scant faith. *If you should have faith as a kernel of mustard, you shall be declaring to this mountain, 'Proceed hence – there!' and it will be proceeding.* NOTHING WILL BE IMPOSSIBLE FOR YOU.

> Note that these words are spoken to the disciples and pertain to the particular era in which they lived. We cannot assume that these words apply to all disciples (followers) in all eras. Observe also that at this point in time the disciples are still lacking in faith.

Jesus again tells of His coming death, *and the third day He will be roused.* The disciples are *tremendously sorry.*

Avoid snaring others (17:24)

The double drachma tax is to be paid by those who are not *sons of the kings of the earth.* Those who are sons do not pay the tax.

Yet, lest we should be snaring them, cast a fish hook into the sea and pick up the first fish coming up, and opening its mouth you will be finding a *stater.* Getting that, give it to them for Me and you.

> So Jesus infers that He and the disciples would not be obligated to pay the tax, as they are *sons of the king.* But the tax is paid nonetheless <u>so as to avoid snaring them</u>. Here is an example of doing something that one is not obligated to do, if by doing so we can avoid snaring others. This reminds us of Paul's teachings on giving up rights that may cause others to stumble. (1 Corinthians 10:23-33)

CHAPTER 18

Humility (18:1)

One cannot enter the kingdom unless he becomes as a little child. He who *humbles* himself as a little child is *greatest in the kingdom.* Whoever receives one such little child in My name, receives Me.

> Using children as the example, Jesus is illustrating the need for humility to enter the Kingdom.

Avoid snaring others (18:5)

It is better to be drowned than to snare one who is believing. Woe to the world because of snares. It is necessary that snares come, but woe to that man thru whom the snare is coming. To remove a snaring member is better than being cast into FIRE EONIAN.

Overview of MATTHEW

> *Fire eonian* is a reference to Gehenna; the Valley of Hinnom. We see that the Kingdom rules will be strictly enforced. Better to take extreme measures to remove sin than to forfeit one's life and to have one's body cast into the Valley of Hinnom.

Parable of the lost sheep (18:10)

If a man has 100 sheep but one is led astray, he will leave the 99 to seek the one. If he finds it he will rejoice over it rather than over the 99. *It is not the will of your Father that one of these little ones should perish.*

> This expresses the heart of the Father; to seek the one who is straying. Will God's heart change? Will He be satisfied to give up on the many who are led astray and who are tormented "endlessly" in a fiery hell?

Procedure when a brother sins against you (18:15)

If a brother is sinning expose him between you and him alone. If he does not hear take one or two others with you. If he disobeys tell it to the ecclesia. If he disobeys the ecclesia consider him as one of the nations.

> Note the contrast between the *nations* and the *ecclesia*, which is comprised at this time of *Israelites*.
>
> As is the case with much we have read in Matthew, this would seem to be a good principle for handling problems within the ecclesia today. But rules for church conduct come from a different age (Paul's writings). The ecclesia in Jesus' day was a different group than in our present era. Then the ecclesia was entirely Jewish, and they were being gathered into the kingdom upon the earth. Today the ecclesia is Gentile and Jew alike without distinction, being gathered into the Body of Christ with an expectation in *the heavenlies*, not upon the earth. These instructions in Matthew are given specifically to the ecclesia of Jesus' day. We cannot automatically carry over this "rule for church conduct" into the ecclesia of the present day.

Authority granted to disciples (18:18)

Those things bound in heaven you should be binding on the earth. Those things loose in the heavens you shall be loosing on the earth. *If ever two of you should be agreeing on the earth concerning any matter, whatsoever it is they should be requesting shall be coming to them from My Father Who is in the heavens. For where two or three are, gathered in My name, there am I in the midst of them.*

> *Where two or three are gathered* ... Does this apply in our present age? We hear this passage quoted often today, but it pertains to the kingdom age. Experience should show us that there are times where two or three agree and the matter does not come to pass. In the kingdom age, where two or three are gathered Christ is in their midst. In the present age, where one is gathered he has the holy spirit of God *in his midst*. As wonderful as the words sound; *where two or three are gathered* ... we have something even better in this present age!

Jesus continues teaching (18:21)

Jesus tells Peter a brother should be pardoned *seventy times seven*.

> Would a God who stresses the need for repeated forgiveness come to the point where He, Himself, will not forgive those being tormented "endlessly" in hell?

In the *parable of the unmerciful servant* the kingdom is likened to a king wanting to settle accounts with his slaves. The king has compassion and forgives his loan. But the slave then goes to a fellow slave and demands payment. The king finds out and has the slave he had forgiven tormented until he pays everything owed. *Was it not binding on you to be merciful to your fellow slave as I am merciful to you? Thus shall My heavenly Father also be doing to you if each one should not be pardoning his brother from your hearts.*

> What do we learn about pardon? Pardon can be retracted. Here it is contingent upon the recipient granting pardon to others. When studying the Scriptures we must take care to OBSERVE THINGS THAT ARE DIFFERENT and not mix them together thru our carelessness. Pardon is something a king (executive) has the authority to grant. Justification, which Paul talks about, is something a judge (judicial) has the authority to grant. Pardon is taking one who is found guilty and suspending their sentence. Justification is finding someone innocent of the charges. There is a big difference.

> In the kingdom age which we read of here in Matthew, pardon is offered. Later, and to a different group of called-out-ones (*ekklesia*), Paul will talk of justification. Let us pay close attention to these details and not assume that things like pardon and justification are the same. Similarly, as we continue our study of the New Testament let us observe the distinction between such things as born again vs. new creation, kingdom of God vs. the heavenlies, and the evangel of the kingdom vs. the evangel of grace.

Overview of MATTHEW

CHAPTER 19

Divorce (19:3)

Many follow Jesus and are healed. He teaches concerning divorce. What God yokes together let not man be separating. The Pharisees ask, Why did Moses direct to give a scroll of divorce? Jesus replies, Moses permits due to hardheartedness. But it was not so from the beginning. Whoever should be dismissing his wife (except for prostitution) and should be marrying another, is committing adultery, and he who marries her who has been dismissed is committing adultery.

> God hates divorce. He prohibits divorce in the Law. But the Law cannot save; it can only show man his inabilities and imperfection. We should not, in the current age, use this section to "enforce" the Law pertaining to divorce, but we should still recognize that God hates divorce.

The disciples ask, Is celibacy preferred? Jesus replies, Not all are containing this saying, but those to whom it has been given. The one able to contain it, let him contain it.

> Not all have the ability to remain celibate. Paul will later advise the believers at Corinth to marry if they cannot control their passions (1 Corinthians 7:9). Experience displays the wisdom in this as we observe many problems within the "priesthood" of the Roman Catholic Church who are required to remain celibate.

Entering the kingdom (19:13)

Let the little children come to Me, for of such is the kingdom of the heavens.

A rich young man asks Jesus, Teacher, what good shall I be doing that I should be having *life eonian?*

Keep the precepts. Do not murder. Don't commit adultery. Do not steal. Do not bear false testimony. Honor thy father and mother. Love your associate as yourself.

These all I maintain. In what am I still deficient?

If you are wanting to be PERFECT ... *sell your possessions and give to the poor, and you will be having treasures in the heavens. Follow me.*

Hearing this, the youth came away sorrowing, for he had many acquisitions.

> To have *life eonian* or life in the age to come is here paralleled with *being perfect*. Throughout Matthew, entering the kingdom (or gaining life in the eon to come) is dependent upon works (obedience).

It is *hard for the rich to enter the kingdom*. It is easier for a camel to be entering through the eye of a needle than for a rich man to be entering into the kingdom of God. *Who, consequently, can be saved?*

> In other words, if it is up to man to meet the requirements of the Law, who can be saved?

With men this is impossible, yet with God all is possible.

> He takes the focus away from the efforts of men, which are insufficient. He places the focus upon the works of God, with Whom all things are possible.
>
> Consider what we have encountered thus far in Matthew. The requirements to enter the kingdom which will be restored upon the earth seem impossible to keep. How can one exhibit *superabounding righteousness* (5:20) or *perfection* (5:48)? Now we read, *With men this is impossible, yet with God all is possible.* Could it be that all we have read thus far has had the purpose of demonstrating to mankind that they are unable to meet the requirements to enter the kingdom, despite the best of intentions and effort? Could God be progressively leading mankind (thus far only Israel) to the point where we understand it is only God's grace that can save us?
>
> WHAT DOES IT MEAN TO BE "SAVED?"
>
> Salvation or being saved, as used throughout God's Word, does not always mean the same thing. Here in the kingdom age it appears that being saved means entering the kingdom when it comes upon the earth. For us within the Body of Christ today, being saved means having an expectation in the heavens when we are called to be with Him, and being saved from the tribulation that is to come upon the earth in the next eon. In the Old Testament being saved often meant being rescued from one's enemies. And at times when one is healed it is said they were *saved* (from their disease; saved from death). Let us pay close attention to the context when salvation or "being saved" are referenced in the Scriptures, to understand what the subject is being saved from and how he is being saved (works, obedience, faith, etc).

Jesus speaks of the rewards for those who follow. When the Son of Man is seated on the throne they will *sit on twelve thrones, judging the twelve tribes of Israel.* Everyone who leaves houses, family, fields on account of My name, a hundred-fold shall you be getting. You shall enjoy the allotment of *life eonian.* Yet many of the first shall be last, and the last first.

> Again we see Jesus' ministry is directed to ISRAEL and not to those of the nations. The kingdom, when restored upon the earth, will see Israel serving as God's instrument to accomplish His will, and the Twelve will reign with Him.
>
> This is fulfilled in Revelation. Throughout Revelation we see a very Jewish character. Paul's "joint heirs" is not referred to, but instead we see the kingdom with preference given to the Jews. This makes sense. The kingdom that was being introduced by Jesus, and later by Peter, is postponed when the Jews continually reject the kingdom message. When the kingdom agenda is temporarily set aside, Paul introduces a new thing; the Body of Christ comprised of Gentile and Jew alike with neither having superiority. (Ephesians 2:11) But in the end times which we see in Revelation, the kingdom agenda returns as God completes His work within the ages. In the final eon we see the righteous Jews upon the earth with Christ reigning upon the throne. The Body of Christ is serving in the heavenly realms, not upon the earth. (Ephesians 2:6, 2 Timothy 2:12, 4:18, 1 Corinthians 6:3)

CHAPTER 20

Parable of the vineyard (20:1)

Those coming in the eleventh hour receive the same pay as those who came first. *Is it not allowed me to do what I want with that which is mine? Thus shall the last be first and the first last.*

Jesus again predicts His death. (20:17)

The mother of Zebedee's sons make a special request of Jesus; for her sons to be seated beside Jesus in the kingdom. *To be seated at My right and My left is not Mine to give.* The one wanting to become great must be a servant. The Son of Man came to serve, and to give His soul *a ransom* for many.

Healing (20:29)

Leaving Jericho, a vast throng follows Jesus. Having compassion, Jesus restores sight to two blind men and they follow Him.

CHAPTER 21

Overview of MATTHEW

Triumphal entry (21:1)

The triumphal entry fulfilled that which was declared through the prophet: Your King is coming to you, meek and mounted on an ass. The throngs cried, Hosanna to the Son of David! Blessed be He Who is coming in the name of the Lord! This is the prophet Jesus, from Nazareth of Galilee.

The money changers are expelled from the Temple. It is written, My house a house of prayer shall be called, yet you are making it a burglars' cave. The blind and lame come to Him in the sanctuary and He cures them. The chief priests and scribes see the marvels, hear the throng, and resent it.

A fig tree withers immediately after Jesus declares, No longer, by any means, may fruit be coming of you *for the eon*. The disciples marvel at how instantly the tree withered, and Jesus tells them, *If you should be having faith and not be doubting ... whatsoever you should be requesting in prayer, believing, you shall be getting.*

> This is a word spoken to the disciples that were with Him at that time. Can we legitimately claim that this promise pertains to us today?
>
> The fig tree appears to be symbolic of Israel as a nation. They were called to be baptized and to bear fruit. Instead they rejected their king repeatedly. Now, near the end of Jesus' life and ministry, He symbolically curses the fig tree (Israel). No fruit would come from Israel in the present eon. Israel will again hear the proclamation concerning the kingdom in Acts, following the crucifixion and resurrection of Christ, but there would be no fruit. The stage is being set for the temporary setting aside of Israel as God's grace is extended to the nations. (Romans 11:25)

The chief priests and elders question Jesus' authority, asking by what authority He acts. Jesus refuses to tell them.

Parables (21:28)

In the *parable of the two sons and the vineyard* a man asks his two children to work in his vineyard. One says no but later regrets and goes to work. One says yes but he does not go.

The tax collectors and prostitutes precede you into the kingdom. You did not believe John, but the tax collectors and prostitutes believe him. You do not even regret subsequently, to believe him.

> Jesus does not say the leaders will *never* get into the Kingdom, but that others will *precede* them.

In the *parable of the wicked vinedressers* a man plants a vineyard and travels, leasing it to farmers. He sends his slaves to get his fruit and the farmers kill one. More slaves are sent and they are driven away. He sends his son and they kill him to get his allotment.

Did you never read in the scriptures, the stone that was rejected by the builders came to be the head of the corner? The kingdom of God will be taken from you and given to a nation producing its fruits.

> This prophesies the setting aside of Israel, with the evangel going to the Gentile nations thru Paul. But the kingdom is not *permanently* taken from Israel as we see from Paul's words. (Romans 11:25) The kingdom that is eventually restored upon the earth in Revelation is clearly Jewish in character.

The chief priests and Pharisees know Jesus is talking about them. They seek to hold Him but they fear the throngs, who hold Jesus as a prophet.

CHAPTER 22

In the *parable of the wedding banquet* the kingdom of the heavens is likened to a king preparing for his son's wedding. He sends his slaves to the invited guests but they won't come. He sends other slaves but they don't come. Some slaves are killed. The king is angry and sends troops. Murderers destroy them and the city is burned. Those invited are not worthy so the call goes out to whoever may be found. The slaves gather all they find, wicked and good. The king notices a man without wedding apparel. *Bind his feet and hands, and cast him into outer darkness. Many are the called, yet few are the chosen.*

> Note that *many* are called into the kingdom. Some refuse to come, and those that do come are judged, with some being cast out of the kingdom. This is a picture of Christ's return to the earth, and the separation between the holy city and those outside the city. (Revelation 21:2; 21:24 - 22:2)

Testing Jesus (22:15)

The Pharisees consult together, planning to trap Jesus. They ask if it is allowed to pay the poll tax to Caesar? Jesus replies, Pay what belongs to Caesar, to Caesar. Pay what belongs to God, to God.

The Sadducees ask Jesus about husbands and wives in the resurrection. *You are deceived, not being acquainted with the scriptures, nor yet with the power of God. In the resurrection they are not marrying, but are as messengers of God in heaven.*

Overview of MATTHEW

> As Jesus speaks of the resurrection, let us consider what the Scriptures say about that subject. Some have their destiny in the coming age (eon) in the earthly kingdom. This includes the many righteous Jews of Old Testament times (e.g. David), the twelve apostles, and those hearing the circumcision evangel (evangel of the kingdom) when it was proclaimed. They look to the resurrection when they will take their place within the kingdom of heaven as it is restored upon the earth. Also included within the earthly kingdom will be those found righteous upon the earth and still living when the Lord returns to reign.
>
> But some have their destiny in the age to come not upon the earth but in the heavenlies. (1 Thessalonians 4) Paul tells of a secret that had been hidden in ages past. He tells of the formation of the Body of Christ, with Jews and Gentiles as joint heirs and of equal status. This is the evangel to be proclaimed today; not the Circumcision (kingdom) evangel which has been temporarily set aside, but the Uncircumcision evangel proclaiming the grace of God, where those believing have a destiny not upon the earth but in the heavenlies. Let us take great care to see differences when they are found within the Word of God, so we do not mix together things that are different and proclaim a confusing and incorrect message.

The greatest commandment (22:34)

A Pharisee asks, What is the great precept in the law? Jesus replies, You shall be loving the Lord your God with your whole heart, and with your whole soul, and with your whole comprehension. This is the great and foremost precept. The second is like it: You shall be loving your associate as yourself. On these two precepts is hanging the whole law and the prophets.

> In other words, the *purpose* of the Law is LOVE for God and for others.

Jesus asks the Pharisees: Whose Son is the Christ? The Pharisees reply, David's. Jesus asks, How then is David calling Him Lord? None could answer Him, and none dared from that day to inquire of Him further.

CHAPTER 23

Woe to the Jewish leaders (23:1)

On Moses' seat are seated the scribes and Pharisees. Do as they say to you, but do not do according to their acts. The Scribes and Pharisees place heavy loads on men's shoulders. They work to be noticed by men, take the first reclining place at dinner, take the front seats in the

Overview of MATTHEW

synagogues and are called *rabbi* by men. None may be called Rabbi, Father or Preceptor. There is one teacher, and all others are brethren. There is one Father, the heavenly. There is one Preceptor, the Christ. The greatest shall be servant. Anyone exalting himself will be humbled, and anyone humbling himself will be exalted.

> So much for those within the organized church "clergy" that are called "Father."

Woe to the scribes and Pharisees, for they are hypocrites. They are:
- ✓ <u>Locking the kingdom</u> of the heavens in front of men
- ✓ Not entering nor letting those entering to enter
- ✓ Making proselytes who become a son of Gehenna
- ✓ Blind guides
- ✓ Taking tithes while leaving the weightier matters of the law
- ✓ Cleansing the outside of the cup and plate, but not the inside
- ✓ Like whitewashed sepulchers (beautiful outside, unclean inside)
- ✓ Sons of those who murder the prophets
- ✓ Serpents and progeny of vipers. *How can you flee from the judging of Gehenna?*
- ✓ Killing, crucifying, scourging and persecuting prophets and wise men

On them shall come all the just blood shed on the earth, and all these things will be arriving on this generation

Jesus laments over Jerusalem (23:37)
How many times do I want to assemble your children, and you will not. You will not be seeing Me till you should be saying, Blessed is He Who is coming in the name of the Lord!

CHAPTER 24

Jesus foretells the end times ("Olivet Discourse") (24:1)
Jesus predicts the destruction of the temple and the disciples ask what will be the sign of His presence and the conclusion of the eon. Jesus replies with what is commonly known as the *Olivet discourse*. He warns them not to be deceived, for many will come saying they are the Christ. They will hear of battles, nation will be roused against nation and kingdom against kingdom, there will be famines and quakes; and these are just the beginning of the pangs. Followers will be given up and afflicted. Many will be snared and will be giving one another up. There will be many false prophets who will deceive many, and there will be a growing lawlessness. The love of many will be cooling. *He who endures to the consummation shall be saved.*

Overview of MATTHEW

The evangel of the kingdom will be heralded to the whole earth as a testimony to all the nations, and *then the consummation will be arriving.*

> Jesus appears to be referring to the fulfillment of what is commonly called the GREAT COMMISSION. (28:16) Note from Jesus' words that this is not something that appears to be imminent in His day, but will occur just prior to His return to the earth.
>
> These events will occur before the end of the age (the *consummation*) but will be preceded by battles, famines, false prophets, etc. During the end times (of which we read in Revelation) Israel will serve as God's instrument upon the earth, proclaiming the kingdom evangel as a testimony to all nations. But today, in our current era, it is not appropriate to proclaim the *evangel of the kingdom.* Yes, this evangel was announced by Jesus, and even later (in Acts) by Peter; but always to ISRAEL. Today the kingdom has been temporarily set aside (Romans 11:25-6) and we within the Body of Christ are to proclaim the evangel God has revealed for this age; the *evangel of the uncircumcision,* the evangel of grace. We have absolutely no authority or commission to proclaim the evangel of the kingdom or the "Great Commission" today.
>
> Jesus proceeds with some details concerning the end time events commonly known as the Great Tribulation (24:15).

When the abomination of desolation as declared through Daniel the prophet is standing in the holy place (Daniel 11:31; 12:11) they are to flee. There will be a great affliction unlike any that occurred before, and unless the days are discounted no flesh at all would be saved. But because of the chosen the days will be discounted.

> The *chosen* refers to Israel which will play a part upon the earth during the ends times, serving as God's instrument.

If anyone says they are the Christ, they are not to be believed. The coming of the true Christ will be as lightning from east to west (i.e. clearly observed).

> The return of Christ will be clearly evident; as lightning from east to west. History records no such event. Christ's return is still an event to be anticipated.

But false christs and false prophets will use great signs and miracles to deceive. After the sun and moon are darkened and the stars fall and

Overview of MATTHEW

the powers of the heavens are shaken, then will appear the sign of the Son of Man in heaven. All the *tribes* shall grieve.

> *Tribes* refer to Israel, often referred to as the twelve tribes, who have opposed Christ. They will see the Son of Man coming on the clouds, (24:30) dispatching His messengers with a loud trumpet, and His chosen from the extremities of the earth will be assembled. The true coming of the Son of Man should not be confused with the claims of the false christs or false prophets.

Parables emphasizing the need to be watchful (24:32)

The *parable of the fig tree* reminds them that summer is near when the bough becomes tender and the leaves sprout, and when these things are observed He [the Son of Man] is near. *By no means may this generation be passing by till all these things should be occurring.*

> These last words seem to indicate that the end would occur during the lifetime of those hearing Jesus speak. But note that these things *should* be occurring in their lifetime, yet because of Israel's hardness they did *not* occur at that time. Jesus did not reveal the "pause" that would occur as Israel continued to reject the coming kingdom during the period described in Acts. As we study Acts and then Paul's letters, we will see that because the kingdom is rejected despite many proclamations, Israel will be temporarily set aside until the full complement of the nations may enter. (Romans 11:25-6)

Despite the signs that will occur (e.g. the fig tree), NO ONE KNOWS THE DAY OR HOUR when the Son of Man will come; not the messengers, nor the Son; but only the Father. The coming of the Son of Man will be as the days of Noah, where there was eating, drinking and marrying until Noah entered the ark. They did not know when the deluge was coming until it came.

> It is interesting that despite these clear instructions there have been many through the years that have been able to deceive by predicting the exact time of Christ's return, often using supposedly Biblical evidence to substantiate their claims.
>
> Be watching for you are not aware on what day your Lord is coming. (24:42) In an hour you are not supposing, the Son of Man is coming. (24:44)

The *parable of the faithful and evil servants* reveals that the faithful slave will be happy when his lord returns and will be placed over all

- 48 -

Overview of MATTHEW

possessions. But the evil slave who mistreats his fellow slaves, thinking the lord will delay in coming, will find his lot with the hypocrites where there will be lamenting and gnashing of teeth.

CHAPTER 25

The *parable of the wise and foolish virgins* likens the kingdom of the heavens to ten virgins coming to meet the bridegroom. Five are stupid and get their torches but have no oil with them. Five are prudent and get oil with their torches. When the clamor occurs those without oil go out to buy some, but those who are ready enter with the bridegroom and the door is locked. When the foolish return with oil the bridegroom tells them, *I am not acquainted with you.* WATCH, *for you are not aware of the day, neither the hour.* (25:13)

> This cannot be "the rapture" (1 Thessalonians 4:13) when Christ *takes up* the Body of Christ. Here in Matthew we read of Christ's return to the earth, gathering and judging and establishing His kingdom upon the earth.

The *parable of the talents* reminds the hearers that they have been entrusted with the Lord's silver as bankers, and when He comes He will recover what is His together with interest. To everyone who has [when the Lord returns] more will be given, yet from the one who has not all will be taken away, and the useless slave will be cast out into outer darkness where there will be lamenting and gnashing of teeth.

> Here the message is to be good and faithful stewards until He returns; whenever that might be.

Jesus foretells His return (The sheep and goats) (25:31)

Jesus shares the *parable of the sheep and goats*. When the Son of Mankind comes in His glory He will be seated on the throne. All nations will be gathered before Him and He will sever the sheep from the kids. The sheep will enjoy the allotment of the kingdom. *As you do it to one of the least of My brethren, you do it to Me.* These (the *just*) come away into LIFE EONIAN. The goats will be sent away cursed into the FIRE EONIAN made ready for the Adversary and his messengers. *As you do it not to one of the least, you do it not to Me.* These shall come away into CHASTENING EONIAN.

> Note that this judgment is based on WORKS, NOT FAITH. No indication is given that this refers to the resurrection. The nations that are upon the earth are gathered by the Son of Man for judgment and they are judged based on how they treated God's chosen people (Israel). The reward (life) and the penalty (chastening) are not endless, but *eonian*.

Overview of MATTHEW

> The word here translated *chastening* is the Greek *kolasis* and it means in all instances a chastening for the good of the subject, as a tree is pruned for the good of the tree. How can it be for the good of the subject if the chastening goes on endlessly? Furthermore, if we examine all instances where the Greek word *aion* is used it is clear that it cannot possibly convey the idea of endlessness.

CHAPTER 26

The last week ^(26:1)

Jesus tells the disciples that Passover is coming after two days and the Son of Mankind will be given up to be crucified. The chief priests and elders gather with the Chief Priest (Caiaphas). They plot against Jesus, planning to lay hold of Him and kill Him, but not at the festival lest a tumult occur among the people. Jesus is anointed and His disciples question the act, saying the money could be given to the poor. Jesus replies, She works an ideal work for Me. You will always have the poor, but you will not always have Me. She does this for My burial. Judas agrees to betray Jesus and the chief priests give him thirty pieces of silver. He begins to seek an opportunity to give Him up.

Jesus shares the Passover meal with His disciples and this particular Passover will become commonly known as the Lord's Supper. Jesus tells them, The Son of Mankind is going away, as it is written concerning Him. Yet woe to that man thru whom the Son of Man is given up! Ideal were it for Him if that man were not born!

Jesus takes the bread, blesses it, breaks it, and gives it to the disciples saying, Take, eat. This is My body. And taking the cup and giving thanks He gives it to them saying, Drink of it all, for this is My blood of the new covenant that is shed for many for the pardon of sins. I will not drink again till I drink it with you in the kingdom.

Jesus tells His disciples that they will all be snared that night. It is written, I shall be smiting the shepherd, and scattered shall be the sheep of the flock. After My rousing I shall be preceding you into Galilee. Peter objects, I will never be snared! But Jesus tells him that before a cock crows, three times Peter will renounce Him. Peter and the others assure Jesus they will not renounce Him under any circumstances.

In Gethsemane Jesus begins to be sorrowful and depressed. He asks the disciples to remain and watch with Him. He falls on His face, praying, My Father, if it is possible, let this cup pass from Me. But not as I will, but as Thou! He finds the disciples drowsing and says to

Overview of MATTHEW

them, You are not strong enough to watch one hour with Me? Watch and pray, lest you may be entering into trial. The spirit, indeed, is eager; yet the flesh is infirm. A second time He prays, My Father, if this cannot pass from Me if I should not drink it, let Thy will be done! Again He finds them drowsing. He prays a third time saying the same and again He comes to the disciples. Are you drowsing furthermore and resting? Near is the hour and the Son of Mankind is being given up into the hands of sinners.

Arrest & trial (26:47)

Judas leads a throng to arrest Jesus. As they lay hands on Him one with Jesus cuts off the ear of the chief priest's slave. Jesus rebukes him saying, All those taking the sword, by the sword will perish. Do you suppose I cannot entreat My Father and have Him send twelve legions of messengers? How, then, may the scriptures be fulfilled; thus it must occur. All His disciples flee.

> The miracles have ceased. Jesus points out that He could summon legions to rescue Him, but He will call for no miracle here. It is the will of the Father that these things take place.

They lead Jesus away to Caiaphas, the chief priest. The scribes and the elders are gathered. Peter follows from afar, entering the chief priest's courtyard. They seek false testimony to put Jesus to death, but cannot find any. They demand, Tell us if you are the Christ, the Son of God. Jesus replies, You say it. You shall be seeing the Son of Mankind sitting at the right hand of power and coming on the clouds of heaven. The chief priest objects, He blasphemes! Liable to death is he. They spit in His face and buffet Him.

Peter disowns Jesus (26:69)

Peter disowns Jesus and is reminded of what Jesus had foretold. He laments bitterly. The chief priests and elders consult to put Him to death.

CHAPTER 27

Trial (27:1)

They take Him to Pontius Pilate the governor. Judas, perceiving He was condemned, is regretting. He turns back the thirty pieces of silver to the chief priests saying, I sinned in giving up innocent blood. Judas strangles himself.

Pilate questions Jesus, You are the king of the Jews? Jesus replies, You are saying it. At being accused by chief priests and elders He answers nothing. The chief priests and elders persuade the throngs to request release of Bar-Abbas, yet to be destroying Jesus. Pilate asks, What, then, shall I be doing with Jesus, who is termed Christ? They call for Him to be crucified. Pilate replies, Innocent am I of the blood of this just man. The people reply, His blood be on us and on our children! Jesus is whipped and given over to be crucified. Soldiers of the governor mock Him and lead Him away to be crucified.

Death & burial (27:32)

They crucify Him at *Golgotha* which is termed *Skull's Place*. They write above His head: *This is Jesus, the King of the Jews*. He is crucified together with two robbers. Those going by blaspheme Him saying, You who are demolishing the temple and building it in three days, save yourself! If you are the Son of God, descend from the cross! If he is king of Israel, let him descend now from the cross, and we will believe on him! The robbers also reproach Him.

Jesus cries out, *Eloi! Eloi! Lema sabachthani?* (My God! My God! Why didst Thou forsake Me?) One pierced His side with a lance head, and out came water and blood.

Jesus, crying with a loud voice, let out the spirit. The curtain of the temple is rent in two. The earth quakes and the rocks are rent. The tombs are opened and many bodies of the reposing saints are roused. A centurion and those with him remark, Truly this was God's Son. Many women are there also, beholding from afar (Mary Magdalene, Mary the mother of James and Joses, the mother of the sons of Zebedee).

Joseph from Arimathea (a rich man and a disciple of Jesus) asks Pilate for the body, and he places it in his new tomb with a large stone at the door. Mary Magdalene and the other Mary sit in front of the tomb. The chief priests and Pharisees go to Pilate. Remembering that Jesus said He would be roused after three days they ask that the sepulcher be secured until the third day, lest the body be stolen with the disciples telling the people He was roused. Pilate assigns a detail to secure the tomb.

CHAPTER 28

Resurrection (28:1)

At the lighting up into *one of the sabbaths*, Mary Magdalene and the other Mary come to the sepulcher.

> *One of the Sabbaths* is often erroneously translated the *first day of the week*, giving the notion that the resurrection occurred on Sunday. There

> is no linguistic warrant to render the translation in this way; it is only carelessness and the contamination of the Scriptures by religious tradition. There is no word in the Greek for first, or day, or week found anywhere in this passage. The problem is the thinking that *Sabbath* always refers to the weekly Sabbath (Saturday), but Leviticus 23 summarizes seven festivals/feasts that are referred to as *special Sabbaths*. Some Sabbaths occur in close proximity. For example, on the tenth day of the seventh month we have the Day of Covering (Atonement) and five days later is another Sabbath; the Festival of Ingathering. The *evening of the Sabbaths* is where an evening ends one Sabbath and begins another. Occasionally a festival falls on the weekly Sabbath, in which case we have a double Sabbath, or *the day of the Sabbaths*. When we see the phrase *one of the Sabbaths* it refers to the series of Sabbaths between Wave Sheaf and Pentecost. In 28:1 we have just concluded Passover a few days earlier, and *one of the Sabbaths* would refer to the regular weekly Sabbath; a Saturday.

A great quake occurs. A messenger of the Lord from heaven rolls away the stone. From fear the keepers quake and become as the dead. A messenger says to the women, He is not here; He was roused. Go, tell His disciples that He was roused from the dead. He is preceding you into Galilee; there you will see Him. As they go, Jesus meets them. They hold His feet and worship Him. Jesus instructs them, Fear not! Go, tell My brethren to come into Galilee, and there they shall see Me. Some of the detail report to the chief priests all that is occurring. The Jewish leaders bribe the soldiers, giving them a considerable sum of silver and telling them to say that His disciples stole the body as they slept. *And this word is blazed abroad by the Jews unto today.*

"The great commission" (28:16)

The eleven disciples go into Galilee, to the mountain where Jesus arranged with them. Jesus tells them, *Given to Me was all authority in heaven and on the earth. Going, then, disciple all the nations, baptizing them into the name of the Father, Son and holy spirit ... teaching them to be keeping all, whatever I direct you. I am with you all the days till the conclusion of the eon!*

> The Greek verb distinguishes between completeness and incompleteness rather than time. *Given to Me was all* authority (28:18) appears to be in the past tense, but this statement is not yet realized. This will be fulfilled when the seventh trumpet sounds (Revelation 11:15) for we read,

> *The kingdom of this world became our Lord's and His Christ's, and He shall be reigning for the eons of the eons.*
>
> WHY DIDN'T THE DISCIPLES CARRY OUT "THE GREAT COMMISSION" AFTER THE RESURRECTION OF CHRIST?
>
> If the disciples thought "The Great Commission" was to be carried out immediately why did they not act accordingly? They did not go to the nations at any time during their ministries. Could it be that they understood it was not yet time to *disciple all the nations* but that this would occur later, as we see in Revelation? This would be consistent with Jesus' description of the end times when He says, *Heralded shall be this evangel of the kingdom in the whole inhabited earth for a testimony to all the nations, and then the consummation shall be arriving.* (24:14)

RECAP

Through the genealogy provided and the many references to Old Testament prophesies fulfilled, Matthew documents that Jesus meets the requirements to be the Son of David, the Messiah (Anointed One), the King and the Son of God.

John the Baptist opens with the proclamation, *Repent! For near is the kingdom of the heavens* (3:1). When Jesus begins His ministry the message is the same. *Repent! For near is the kingdom of the heavens* (4:12).

In the "Sermon on the Mount" (5:13) Jesus provides specific rules to be observed and enforced when the kingdom is restored upon the earth. The kingdom is *near*, and He is preparing Israel to enter once it is restored.

Matthew records many healings and miracles, and there is a close relationship between the evangel of the kingdom and these miracles.

When Jesus commissions the Twelve they are to go *only to the lost sheep of ISRAEL* (10:6) and they are to proclaim the same message: *Near is the kingdom of the heavens*. He reiterates to the Canaanite woman asking for her daughter's healing: *I was not commissioned except for the lost sheep of Israel.* (15:24)

As opposition from the Jewish leaders builds, Jesus begins to speak only in parables, thereby "locking" the kingdom to all except those to whom He chooses to reveal. He tells the Jewish leaders they were *locking* the kingdom. (23:13) Peter will be given the *keys* of the kingdom (16:19) and we will later see him use these keys to unlock the kingdom in Acts.

Overview of MATTHEW

And so throughout Matthew there is a distinctive Jewish focus. Many Old Testament references are made as Matthew shows his fellow Israelites that Jesus meets all necessary requirements for being the Messiah. Jesus comes to announce the restoration of the kingdom. But the king and the kingdom are rejected by the Jews who so anxiously awaited their coming, and the king is crucified.

Still, the evangel remains the same in the book of Acts when Peter (who was given the keys to the kingdom) proclaims the same message. Christ has been crucified and resurrected, but in the book of Acts it is still the kingdom to come upon the earth that is being proclaimed, and it is proclaimed exclusively to the Jews as was the case throughout Matthew. Salvation, or life in the eon to come, is life in the kingdom of the heavens when it comes upon the earth with Christ upon the throne. But again throughout Acts we see the evangel of the kingdom rejected. When the kingdom is *finally* rejected at the end of Acts, the Jews (and the kingdom evangel) are set aside for a season and the uncircumcision evangel is declared to Jew and Gentile alike without distinction or preference. But have the Jews lost their chance? Has "The Church" taken their place? Paul tells us that Israel has been calloused UNTIL *the complement of the nations may be entering,* after which time *all Israel shall be saved.* (Romans 11:25)

Matthew tells us of a time when the kingdom to come upon the earth was proclaimed to the Jews. Acts continues that message, even after the death and resurrection of Christ. As Acts ends Paul tells us that a new evangel is going out to Jew and Gentile alike. But when this present age has ended the kingdom evangel will once again be proclaimed upon the earth, and we see this happen in Revelation.

When comparing the four gospel accounts there are 30 sections unique to Matthew, all more or less having to do with Matthew's objective in writing; the king and the kingdom. "The kingdom of heaven" occurs 32 times and is not in any other gospel. The phrase makes reference to Daniel's prophecy. (Daniel 2:44; 7:27) "That it might be fulfilled" occurs 9 times and not in the other gospels. "That which was spoken" or "it was spoken" occurs 14 times and nowhere else. Matthew contains 60 references to the Old Testament.

Overview of MATTHEW

Matthew
"The gospel according to Matthew"

Birth of Jesus 1:1
- Lineage (1:1) – Jesus meets the prophetic requirements to be Messiah
- Birth of Jesus (1:18)

John the Baptist proclaims the kingdom 3:1
- "Repent, for *near* is the kingdom" (3:3) – The kingdom evangel
- "Produce fruit worthy of repentance" (3:9)
- "Who warns you to flee from the impending indignation?" (3:7)
- *[Repentance and fruit (works) called for ... indignation coming.]*

Jesus proclaims the kingdom evangel to Israel 2:1
- "Repent for *near* is the kingdom" (4:17)
- Heralding "**evangel of the kingdom**" (4:23)
- Rules for the kingdom – aka "Sermon on the Mount" (5:1)
- Teaching, heralding, curing (4:23)
- Miracles accompany heralding (8-9)
- Pharisees criticize (9:11,34)

Jesus commissions the Twelve 10:1
- "**To the lost sheep of Israel**" (10:6)
- Say: "*Near* **is the kingdom**" (10:7) – The kingdom evangel
- Authority to heal, raise, cleanse, cast out demons
- *[Kingdom near – to be restored to Israel – physical land promised – physical healing & miracles]*

Pharisees plan to kill Jesus 12:14
- Jesus picks grain on Sabbath (12:1)
- Pharisees plan to kill Jesus (12:14)
- Jesus heals on Sabbath (12:9)
- Pharisees ask for a sign (12:38)

Jesus speaks in parables 13:1
- "To you is given to know the secrets of the kingdom, yet to those it has not been given" (13:11)
- "That they are not observing ... hearing ... understanding" (13:13)
- Jesus speaks concerning the kingdom only in parables (13:34)
- *[The kingdom has been "LOCKED" as Jesus taught only using parables]*

On this rock will I build my ecclesia 16:18
- I will give you the "KEYS" of the kingdom (16:19)
- Jesus predicts His death (16:21; 17:24)
- Authority to bind/loose given to the disciples (18:18)

What shall I do to have life eonian? 19:16
- Keep commands; love associate as self
- If wanting to be perfect, sell possession ... give to poor ... follow me
- Hard for the rich to enter the kingdom (19:23)
- "Who, then, can be saved?" (19:25)
- "With men this is IMPOSSIBLE, yet with God all is possible" (19:26)
- *[Speaks of entering the kingdom when restored to Israel.]*

The greatest commandment 22:34
- Love the Lord your God with your whole heart – love associate as yourself
- On these two precepts is hanging the whole law and the prophets

Woe to the Jewish leaders 23:1
- Do not do according to their acts (23:3)
- Placing heavy loads on men's shoulders
- "LOCKING the kingdom of the heavens in front of men" (23:13)

Jesus speaks of the end of the eon 24:1
- What is the sign of Thy presence & the conclusion of the eon? (24:3)
- Affliction, killing, wars -- great tribulation (24:15)
- He who endures to the consummation shall be saved (24:13)
- *[Saved = Life in the kingdom when Christ restores it unto Israel.]*
- Heralded shall be this **evangel of the kingdom** in the whole inhabited earth (24:14)
- Coming of the Son of man (24:29)
- Parable of sheep & goats ... judging those living within the nations when Christ returns (25:31)

Crucifixion & Resurrection 26:1
- Plot against Jesus (26:1)
- Gethsemane (26:36)
- Crucifixion (27:32)
- Resurrection (28:1)

Overview of MATTHEW

Great Commission to the Twelve   28:16
- Disciple all the nations (fulfilled during the Tribulation period found in Revelation)
- *[Command for Israel to take the evangel to the nations – not yet fulfilled as Israel now "set aside."]*

Be going to the lost sheep of the house of Israel (10:6)
I was not commissioned except for the lost sheep of the house of Israel (15:24)

Mark

An Overview of the Scriptures, by
BOB EVELY © 2018.
An Independent Minister of Christ Jesus,
Of the church at Wilmore, Kentucky

Having followed the footsteps of our Lord thru the eyes of Matthew, let us now turn to Mark's account. We will not expect to see a repeat of Matthew; why the need for a second duplicate narrative? Matthew's objective was to prove that the qualifications for Messiah and King had been met in Jesus. Let us now seek to understand Mark's purpose in writing.

CHAPTER 1

The beginning of the evangel (1:1)

The beginning of the evangel of Jesus Christ, Son of God, as it is written in Isaiah the prophet.

> For Mark the *beginning* of the good news is the ministry of John the Baptist. No genealogy! No birth narrative! For Matthew these elements were crucial. But Mark obviously has no need for these elements to satisfy *his* purpose.

John the Baptist (1:2)

I am dispatching My messenger before Thy face, who shall be constructing Thy road in front of Thee. (Malachi 3:1)

The voice of one imploring: 'In the wilderness make ready the road of the Lord! Straight ... be making the highways of Him! (Isaiah 40:3)

> A word from two prophets introduces the story of John the Baptist.

John comes HERALDING A BAPTISM OF REPENTANCE FOR THE PARDON OF SINS. He baptizes those who come confessing their sins. He announces that One will come after him Who is stronger, Who will baptize in holy spirit while John can baptize only in water.

> Paul will later teach that there is only *one* baptism (Ephesians 4:5). In John's day baptism is of water, but he speaks of a day when a *new* baptism will come; a baptism of holy spirit.

Overview of MARK

Jesus is baptized by John, and as He steps out of the water He sees the heavens rent and the spirit as a dove descends and remains on Him. A voice from out of the heavens declares, *Thou art My Son, the Beloved; in Thee I delight.*

Trial in the wilderness (1:12)

The spirit *ejects* Jesus into the wilderness and He undergoes *trial by Satan* for forty days.

> *Satan* is a transliteration of the Hebrew word *satan* which means adversary. In Matthew's account of this same episode we see the word *diabolos* which is the Greek equivalent of the Hebrew *satan*, and which also means adversary.

Jesus heralds the evangel of the kingdom (1:14)

After John's death, Jesus comes into Galilee HERALDING THE EVANGEL OF THE KINGDOM OF GOD. *Fulfilled is the era, and near is the kingdom of God! Repent, and believe in the evangel!*

> Observe that the kingdom is *near*. It is not yet *here*. And the message concerning the kingdom is closely associated with REPENTANCE and BELIEVING in the news that Jesus is proclaiming. For Israel it is not simply a matter of *faith* or *belief*, but *repentance* and a changed *behavior* (works) to become ready to enter the kingdom when it is restored upon the earth.

Disciples called (1:16)

Jesus calls disciples to follow; Simon and Andrew, James and John. He teaches in the synagogue and those hearing are astonished for He teaches as One having authority, not as the scribes.

Healings (1:23)

In the synagogue Jesus casts an unclean spirit out of a man. The audience is in awe, noting the authority Jesus has -- to cause the spirits to obey Him. Tidings concerning Him spread into the whole country about Galilee.

He heals Simon's mother-in-law who was sick with a fever. The crowd brings to Jesus all who have an illness or demons. He *cures* many and He casts out many demons. But He does not let the demons speak *for they were aware that He is the Christ.*

Overview of MARK

> Why? Could it be that the timing is not yet right? Or perhaps it is because He wants the people to recognize Him as the Christ through His own words and works, and not thru the testimony of demons.

The purpose of His ministry (1:35)

He rises early and goes to a desolate place to pray. When the disciples find Him and report that all are seeking Him, Jesus replies, *We may be going elsewhere, into the next towns, that there also I should be* HERALDING; for FOR THIS I CAME OUT.

> Observe; His ministry is not for the purpose of healing and casting out demons but to HERALD His message. This primary mission is *accompanied* by healing and the casting out of demons. Miracles will validate His identity and authority, but HIS PURPOSE IS TO *HERALD* the message He is commissioned to PROCLAIM. And remember that His message concerns *the evangel of the kingdom of God.* (1:14) The kingdom is *near*.
>
> Think back to the days of David and Solomon when the kingdom established by God was at its peak. But then came division and rebellion and exile. The prophets promised restoration of the kingdom and a return to the land. This is the expectation of Israel. Now comes the Son of God (Jesus) to prepare the sheep of Israel to enter the kingdom when it is restored. It is near, and His evangel is intended to prepare Israel. Repentance and belief are closely tied to the message. Will Israel believe as He heralds this good news? Will they repent and prepare themselves to enter the coming kingdom?

He goes into the synagogues in all of Galilee, heralding and casting out demons.

Healings (1:40)

Jesus cleanses a leper and instructs him not to say anything to anyone but to go to the priest to be declared clean. But the leper tells others, and word of his cleansing spreads so that Jesus can no longer enter a city but must remain outside in desolate places. They come to Him from everywhere.

> Could this be the reason He did not want word to spread concerning His miraculous deeds, as it impairs His ability to move about and continue the proclamation of His message?

CHAPTER 2

Overview of MARK

Jesus heals a paralytic who is lowered into the house. He sees their faith and says to the paralytic, *pardoned you are your sins.* Some scribes reason in their hearts that Jesus blasphemes as only God can pardon sins. Jesus recognizes in His spirit what they are thinking and He replies, *What is easier, to be saying to the paralytic, Pardoned are your sins, or to be saying, Rouse and pick up your pallet and walk?* He instructs the paralytic to rouse and walk, and he is healed. All are amazed and glorify God.

Jesus comes out beside the sea and teaches the throng.

> Again we pause and take notice that Jesus' ministry consists of *proclaiming*, and His proclaiming is closely connected with healings and casting out demons which validate His authority.

Opposition (2:14)

He passes the tribute office and calls Levi to follow. They meet at Levi's house where tribute collectors and sinners gather along with Jesus' disciples. The scribes question why Jesus would eat and drink with tribute collectors and sinners and He replies, *No need have the strong of a physician, but those having an illness. I did not come to call the just, but sinners.*

Jesus is questioned why His disciples do not fast as the disciples of John and the Pharisees. Jesus replies that there is no need for the sons of the bridal chamber to fast when the bridegroom is with them, but days will come when the bridegroom is taken away and they *will* fast.

He tells them that no one would sew an unshrunk patch on an old cloak, as this would cause an even larger tear in the cloak. Likewise no one would put fresh wine into old wine skins as it would burst the wine skins. Fresh wine is put into *new* wine skins.

The Pharisees question why Jesus' disciples pluck ears of corn on the sabbath as it is not allowed. But Jesus reminds them that David ate holy bread which was only permitted for the priests. *The sabbath came because of mankind, and not mankind because of the sabbath, so that the Son of Mankind is Lord of the sabbath.*

> Observe that Jesus is referred to here as the Son of Man, emphasizing His solidarity with mankind. This hints at Mark's singular purpose in providing his account.

CHAPTER 3

Overview of MARK

In the synagogue Jesus heals a man with a withered hand. To His critics He asks, *Is it allowed on the Sabbath to do good or to do evil, a soul to save or to kill?* The Pharisees consult with the Herodians to destroy Him.

> The game is afoot. Jesus proclaims the message entrusted to Him, preparing Israel for the coming kingdom. But the leaders of Israel work against Him and now seek to destroy Him.

Jesus retires with His disciples to the sea and a vast multitude from Galilee follow Him. He warns those who were healed not to make Him manifest.

Disciples called (3:13)
Of the disciples He names twelve *apostles* that they may be with Him and that He may COMMISSION them to HERALD, to have authority to CURE DISEASES and to CAST OUT DEMONS. He gives *Simon* the name Peter, and *James* and *John* He names Boanerges, or Sons of Thunder. The remaining apostles are *Andrew, Philip, Bartholomew, Matthew, Thomas, James* of Alpheus, *Thaddeus, Simon* the Canaanite and *Judas* Iscariot who gives Him up.

Opposition (3:22)
The scribes say that Jesus is controlled by Beelzeboul and that He is casting out demons by the chief of demons. He replies in parables, saying to them, *How can Satan be casting out Satan? If a kingdom is parted against itself it is not able to stand. If Satan rose against himself and is divided, he would not be able to stand and would be finished. But no one is able to enter the house of the strong one to plunder his gear, if ever he should not first be binding the strong one. And then he will be plundering his house.*

The unpardoned sin (3:28)
All shall be pardoned the sons of mankind, the penalties of the sins and the blasphemies ... yet whoever should be blaspheming against the holy spirit is having no pardon for the eon, but is liable to the eonian penalty for the sin – for they said, An unclean spirit has he.

> What is the unpardoned sin (commonly called the "unpardonable" sin)? Observe from this context that it is the failure to recognize the holy spirit at work, and instead to credit the work to another (an unclean

spirit). Yet even this sin carries an *eonian* penalty (i.e. for the eon or eons) and not an endless or "eternal" penalty.

When Jesus is informed that His mother and brothers have come He replies, *whoever should be doing the will of God, this one is My brother and sister and mother.*

CHAPTER 4

Parables ^(4:1)

Beside the sea Jesus teaches many things in parables. The *parable of the sower* reveals that much of the seed (the word) is snatched up by Satan or ignored by those who are more concerned with the worries of this eon and the seduction of riches. But some assent to the word and bear much fruit.

When His disciples ask about the parables He tells them: *To you the secret of the kingdom of God has been given, yet to those outside, all is occurring in parables, that, observing, they may be observing and may not be perceiving, and hearing, they may be hearing and not be understanding, lest at some time they should be turning about, and they may be pardoned the penalties of their sins.*

> Observe that the purpose of parables is not to teach in a way that makes the message easier to understand. The purpose is to CONCEAL. But why would Jesus not want *all* to understand and turn about (repent) and be pardoned? Could it be that to enter the kingdom the Lord wants only those who are willing to set aside the things of this world and focus on the things of God? Still, it is interesting that even His closest followers did not understand the meaning of the parable of the sower until Jesus explained it to them.

In rapid succession we see two short parables. *The lamp* is not coming to be hidden, but to be placed on a lampstand. Nothing is hidden except it will be manifested. And *beware what you are hearing; how you measure it.* He who has, more will be given. But he who has not, even what he has will be taken from him.

In the *parable of the harvest* the kingdom of God is likened to seed cast on the earth. The seed grows when the man is not aware, and when it becomes fruit it is harvested.

In the *parable of the mustard seed* the seed is very small but it becomes greater than all the greens.

Jesus speaks in parables; yet privately He explains all to His disciples.

A miracle (4:35)

While on the ship a storm comes and Jesus *calms the sea*. But He rebukes the disciples. *Why are you so timid? How is it you have no faith?* The disciples are afraid and ask one another who Jesus is that even the wind and sea obey Him?

> It seems this is a part of their training process. The disciples learn that Jesus not only has the authority and ability to bring healing; He also has authority over the laws of nature.

CHAPTER 5

Healings (5:1)

In Gergesenes Jesus *casts out an unclean spirit* from a man who had been living among the tombs. When the man first sees Jesus he runs and WORSHIPS Him, acknowledging that He is the Son of God and asking that Jesus not torment him.

> So *worship* need not occur in a "holy place" or in a corporate setting. Here there is no assembly. There is no music. Study the word *worship* throughout the Scriptures and you will find that it simply means a "coming toward" the object of worship. There is no need to "go to church" to worship.
>
> Observe also that even unclean spirits recognize Jesus as the Son of God, and they acknowledge His authority over the spirit realm. And it is revealing that when Jesus casts the spirits into a herd of hogs which immediately run into the sea and are drowned, the herders ask Jesus to leave the area. They are more concerned with the temporal (their herd of hogs) than with the Son of God.

The demoniac wants to leave with Jesus on the ship but Jesus tells him to return home and report *whatever the Lord has done for you and how He is merciful to you*. When the man does so, all who hear these things in Decapolis marvel.

As throngs follow Jesus everywhere He goes, a woman is healed who has had a hemorrhage for twelve years and who simply touches His cloak. Having felt the power go out of Him, Jesus says to the woman, *Daughter, your faith has SAVED you.*

Overview of MARK

> What does *saved* mean in this context? Saved from what? The woman is saved from her disease and therefore she is saved from death which would result from her disease. When we encounter the word *saved* we must always ask; what is the person being saved from? What does "saved" mean in this context?

Jairus, a chief of the synagogue whose daughter has taken ill, approaches Jesus and asks that He come and SAVE his daughter. By the time Jesus arrives the girl has died, but Jesus replies: *Do not fear. Only believe.* Jesus enters the house with only Peter, James and John, and tells those inside that *the little girl did not die, but is drowsing.*

> While the child had literally died, Jesus relates death to sleep; something that is not permanent as it, too, is overcome by the power of God.

Some inside ridicule Jesus at His words, and He ejects those that do so. Jesus tells the girl to *rouse*, and she rises and walks about. After Jesus restores life to Jairus' daughter He cautions them not to tell anyone.

> Why would Jesus ask the demoniac to return home and tell everyone what had happened, yet to those observing the restoration of Jairus' daughter He cautions not to tell anyone? Might we deduce that while He is still in the area Jesus does not want the word to grow too quickly as it would prevent Him from continuing with His ministry and mission in that vicinity?

CHAPTER 6

In His own country (6:1)

In His own country Jesus teaches in the synagogue. The majority is astonished at His wisdom and powerful deeds, but they are snared. Is He not the artisan; the son of Mary? Is He not the brother of James, Joseph, Judas and Simon? Jesus says to them, *A prophet is not dishonored except in his own country and among his relatives and in his home.* He *could not do any powerful deeds there* except curing a few who are ailing.

> Miracles seem to be connected with belief. As belief in Jesus and the coming kingdom message grows, miracles increase. But as doubt enters, miracles decrease.

He continues about the villages around, teaching.

Overview of MARK

Commissioning of the Twelve (6:7)

He gives to the Twelve authority over unclean spirits, and He sends them out two by two. They are to take nothing with them. If any do not receive them or hear them they are to leave. More tolerable will it be for Sodom and Gomorrah in the day of judging than for that city.

> Observe that this commissioning and authority is given only to the Twelve and not to all disciples or all who believe. We must take care not to extend directives or promises to a broader group (such as "the church") when they were made to a specific group in a specific era. This is what Paul meant when He instructed the ecclesia to "rightly divide" God's Word. (2 Timothy 2:15)

The Twelve go out *heralding* and *calling for repentance*. They cast out many demons and cure many by rubbing them with oil. Herod hears these things and believes John the Baptist has been roused from the dead, for John had been beheaded by Herod's order. Others think it is Elijah or one of the prophets.

Miracles (6:35)

Jesus multiplies five cakes of bread and two fishes to *feed 5000*. He *walks on the water*. At first His disciples think He is a phantom and are afraid. When He comes aboard the ship the wind flags and they are amazed. They had not understood as to the bread; their heart was calloused. In Gennesaret any having an illness were brought to Him. Wherever He went, *all who touched His cloak were saved*.

CHAPTER 7

Criticism (7:1)

Pharisees and scribes come from Jerusalem and ask why His disciples are not walking in accord with the tradition of the elders, as they do not wash their hands before eating. But the Pharisees and scribes had repudiated the precepts of God while holding the tradition of men. They *invalidate* the word of God by their tradition.

> Observe this lesson concerning the precepts of God as contrasted with the traditions of men, and consider the contrast between the precepts of God and the religious rules and teachings within the organized churches of our day. How many things are taught in churches today as being precepts of God, when in fact they are traditions of men? Drinking? Smoking? Baptism requirements? Sabbath keeping for the

Body of Christ? Church-going? Are these based on a correct, "rightly divided" (2 Timothy 2:15) interpretation of the Scriptures, or man-made traditions?

That which comes out of a man contaminates him (7:14)

Jesus tells the throng that nothing outside of a man can contaminate him by going in – only those things going out of a man contaminate him. His disciples later ask about the meaning of this parable. Jesus explains that the things taken into the man are processed and the waste expelled. But that coming out of a man comes from his heart – *evil reasonings, prostitutions, thefts, murders, adulteries, greed, wickedness, guile, wantonness, a wicked eye, calumny, pride, imprudence.* (7:22-23)

> So while we see different "administrations" in the Scriptures from one era to the next, this list would seem to be representative of things that are inappropriate behaviors in God's eyes in any era.

Miracles – including one that benefits a non-Israelite (7:24)

In the frontiers of Tyre and Sidon a Greek woman from Syro-Phoenicia brings her daughter with an unclean spirit to Jesus. He says to her, *Let first the children be satisfied, for it is not ideal to take the children's bread and cast it to the puppies.* The woman notes that even puppies eat scraps from under the table, and Jesus responds by casting the out the demon.

> Observe that the actions of Jesus have benefited a Gentile, but only after resistance on His part. HE HAD COME FOR THE SHEEP OF ISRAEL. That was His commission. This does not mark a new direction for Jesus' ministry, as He will continue to go strictly to the sheep of Israel. But because of this woman's faith and persistence, in this instance she is granted the healing she requests. In the era of Jesus' earthly ministry, Gentiles are only benefactors of His ministry indirectly; because of Israel. They receive, as this woman puts it, scraps from under Israel's table.

Jesus heals a deaf stammerer and instructs those witnessing to tell no one, but they herald it more exceedingly.

CHAPTER 8

He feeds 4000. The Pharisees ask for a sign, *trying Him;* but no sign is given.

Overview of MARK

Beware of the leaven (8:14)

Beware of the leaven of the Pharisees and the leaven of Herod. They think Jesus is speaking of literal bread and point out they have nothing to eat. *Why are you reasoning that you have no bread? Not as yet are you apprehending, neither understanding? Still calloused is your heart? Having eyes, are you not observing? And having ears, are you not hearing?*

> At this point in the journey the disciples still fail to understand the message Jesus is proclaiming thru word and deed, and they continue to require explanation from the Lord.

A healing (8:22)

A blind man is healed.

Who do you say that I am? (8:27)

Some are saying He is John the Baptist, some Elijah, and others that He is one of the prophets. Jesus asks, *Who are you saying that I am?* Peter replies, *Thou art the Christ, the Son of God.* And He tells them not to tell anyone.

> Jesus has tested the waters. Are the disciples beginning to grasp His identity after hearing His words and seeing the miraculous deeds? Immediately Jesus begins preparing them for what lies ahead.

Jesus foretells His death and resurrection (8:31)

The Son of Mankind must be suffering much and be rejected by the elders and the chief priests and the scribes, and be killed and after three days rise. Peter objects.

> Peter's objection stems from the highest of motives. He does not want His Lord to suffer and die. But despite his motives, Peter is rebuked.

Go behind Me satan! for you are not disposed to that which is of God but that which is of men.

> Remember that *satan* means *adversary*. When Peter wishes to implement his own intentions in place of the intentions of God, he is acting as an adversary to God.

The cost of following (8:34)

If anyone is wanting to come after Me, let him renounce himself and pick up his cross and follow Me. For whosoever may be wanting to save his soul will be destroying it, yet whoever shall be destroying his soul on account of Me and of the evangel will be saving it. For what is it benefiting a man to gain the whole world and forfeit his soul?

> The *soul* is the consciousness aspect of life. The soul was generated when God took mere soil and animated it with His spirit. Joining the spirit and soil to create the soul (consciousness/life) might be compared with applying electricity to a filament to produce light.
>
> To gain the world (worldly gain) and forfeit the soul (conscious life) refers to forfeiting life in the eon/age to come when Christ restores the kingdom upon the earth. But this does not mean the offender will forfeit life at a future time when all is restored at the end of the eons as described in 1 Corinthians 15 when God becomes All in all.

CHAPTER 9

Transfiguration (9:1)

Jesus tells the disciples, There are some of those standing here who under no circumstances should be tasting death till they should be perceiving the kingdom of God having come in power. Peter, James and John witness the transfiguration and hear a voice from out of the cloud saying, *This is My Son, the Beloved. Hear Him.* Jesus tells them to tell no one until the Son of Mankind arises from the dead.

Healing (9:14)

A man with an unclean spirit approaches Jesus and asks, If Thou art in any way able to help us ... But Jesus asks the man, Why the if? You are able to believe. All is possible to him who is believing. And the man responds, I am believing! Help my unbelief! Jesus casts out the unclean spirit, which His disciples had been unable to do. Jesus tells them, This species can come out by nothing except prayer.

Who is the greatest? (9:33)

On the road the disciples argue who is the greatest. If anyone is wanting to be first, he will be last of all and servant of all. Whoever should be receiving one of such little children in My name is receiving Me, and whoever may be receiving Me is not receiving Me, but Him Who commissions Me.

> Here we see Mark's unique perspective as shared in his gospel account ... to portray Jesus as a servant. We also note from these words that Jesus

Overview of MARK

> is not acting on His own or in accord with His own will. He is acting in accord with God the Father Who has commissioned Him.

Some who are casting out demons are not followers. Jesus tells His disciples not to forbid them, for he who is not against us is for us.

Don't be a snare (9:42)

Jesus warns against snaring the little ones who are believing. It is better to cut off one's hands, feet or eyes than to be cast into Gehenna and the *unextinguished fire*.

> Observe that these words pertain to those hoping to enter the kingdom when it is restored upon the earth. This has nothing to do with faith; it is entirely works-based. Observe also that it is not an "unquenchable fire" but a fire that is, for the time period mentioned, *unextinguished*. And note that Gehenna is not "hell" as found in many Bible translations, but a physical location outside of Jerusalem that is used as a landfill and where fires continue to burn (the Valley of Hinnom).

CHAPTER 10

Jesus is tested (10:1)

The Pharisees test Jesus regarding divorce. Jesus points out that the precept permitting divorce that came thru Moses was a concession because of man's hardheartedness, *Yet from the beginning of creation God makes them male and female. On this account a man will be leaving his father and mother and will be joined to his wife, and the two will be one flesh. ... What God, then, yokes together, let not man be separating.*

> So God's desire is for there to be no divorce, though it is permitted within the Law due to man's hardheartedness. While the Body of Christ is not under the Law (it was given only to Israel), and while those who have been divorced should not be judged, it is obvious that God's desire is for there to be <u>no divorce</u>. And we also observe here that marriage is <u>between a man and a woman</u>, not two of the same sex.

Let the children come to me (10:13)

Do not forbid them, for of such is the kingdom of God. Whoever should not be receiving the kingdom of God as a little child, may under no circumstances be entering into it.

Overview of MARK

The rich man ^(10:17)
A rich man asks Jesus what he must do to be *enjoying the allotment of life eonian*. Despite the fact that he is keeping the precepts, Jesus tells the man he still lacks one thing: *Go. Whatever you have, sell, and be giving to the poor, and you will be having treasure in heaven*. But the man went away in sorrow, for he had many acquisitions. *Easier is it for a camel to pass through the eye of a needle than for a rich man to be entering into the kingdom of God*. The disciples ask, then, WHO CAN BE SAVED? *With men it is impossible, but not with God, for all is possible with God*.

> It would seem that the requirements to enter the kingdom are so difficult that none can enter, which prompts the question from His disciples. Could this be displaying to us the real reason for the law and precepts ... to show man his inability to meet the standards of righteousness and to cause him to see the need for God's grace?

Reward for those making sacrifices ^(10:28)
Those who leave houses, family, fields on My account and on account of the evangel ... will be having *life eonian* in the *coming eon*.

> Observe carefully the word structure. *The coming eon* shows us clearly that an eon (*aion* in the Greek) is a finite period of time. It is inferred that we are in the midst of an eon and there is a *coming eon*. *Life eonian* refers to life in the eon that is to come. Jesus had come to proclaim the coming kingdom to Israel, and those that made sacrifices for His sake and for the sake of the evangel (the good news concerning the coming kingdom) would have life in the coming eon when the kingdom is established upon the earth.

Going to Jerusalem - He tells of His impending death ^(10:33)
The Son of Mankind will be given up to the chief priests and the scribes, and they will be condemning Him to death; and He will be raised after three days.

James and John ask to be seated on either side of Jesus when He comes in His glory, but Jesus tells them it is not His to give such a reward. This authority belongs to the Father. Furthermore, it is not as with the chiefs of the nations. *For even the Son of Mankind came, not to be served, but to serve, and to give His soul a ransom for many*.

> To give His *soul*. If we think that losing one's soul is a permanent condition that results in the soul spending eternity in the torments of hell, look closely here. Jesus gave His soul as a ransom; yet He did not lose His soul for eternity in the process. To lose one's soul simply means to lose one's life, as the soul is the consciousness aspect of life. Jesus gave up His soul (life) in the present age when He was crucified; but He regained His soul (life) when resurrected by the power of God. Also observe in these words the purpose for which Mark writes. *The Son of Mankind came not to be served, but to serve.* The Son of Man is a servant. Those who follow are to have a servant's heart.

A healing (10:46)

Jesus heals a blind man (Bar-Timeus).

CHAPTER 11

Triumphal entry (11:1)

Jesus makes His triumphal entry into Jerusalem. Many followers proclaim, Blessed be THE COMING KINGDOM OF OUR FATHER DAVID in the name of the Lord!

> This was the expectation of Israel. Not "going to heaven" but a restoration of David's kingdom. Not a kingdom that was already in place, but the kingdom to come upon the earth "as it is in heaven."

Jesus curses a fig tree that has nothing but leaves. And though it was not the season of figs, Jesus tells them, By no means may anyone still be eating fruit of you *for the eon.*

> This appears to be a figurative reference to Israel's rejection of the kingdom. There would be no fruit in the present eon. It would not be until the eon to come, when Christ returns and establishes the kingdom upon the earth, that there would be fruit.

Those buying and selling Jesus casts out of the sanctuary.

The chief priests and scribes seek how to destroy Jesus because they fear Him, for the entire throng is astonished at His teaching.

Along the way the disciples see the fig tree that Jesus had cursed. It was withered from the roots, and they are amazed. Jesus instructs them, *If you have faith of God, verily, I am saying to you that whosoever may be saying to this mountain, Be picked up and cast into the sea, and may not be doubting in his heart, but should be believing that what he*

Overview of MARK

is speaking is occurring, it shall be his, whatsoever he may be saying. Therefore I am saying to you, All, whatever you are praying and requesting, be believing that you obtained, and it will be yours. Jesus also instructs them that when praying they must forgive, else the Father will not forgive them.

> These instructions for faith and prayer are not a blank check for all peoples in all ages ... that whatever is asked for will be received as long as there is unwavering faith. Jesus was speaking TO THE TWELVE. And these remarks are related to the coming kingdom; a kingdom that will physically come upon the earth, where earthly healings, signs and wonders were a part of the evangel being proclaimed. But later, in Paul's ministry, when Israel is temporarily set aside and when Paul shares the evangel intended for the Body of Christ, grace is sufficient. Within the Body of Christ our expectation is not the kingdom to come upon the earth, but we await our Lord's call to join Him in the heavens where we will serve Him. Logically, earth-bound signs and wonders do not relate to the evangel intended for the Body of Christ in our present era. Our expectation is not upon this earth as is the case with Israel.

The chief priests and scribes challenge Jesus: By what authority are you doing these things? He refuses to respond to their question.

CHAPTER 12

Parable of the vineyard (12:1)

The farmers mistreat the owner's servants and kill his son. Therefore the owner will destroy the farmers and will give the vineyard to others. They seek to hold Jesus but are afraid of the throng, for they understood that the parable referred to them.

Jesus tested (12:13)

The Pharisees test Jesus regarding the poll tax. The Sadducees test Jesus regarding the resurrection. A scribe tests Him regarding the most important precept. When the scribe agrees that Jesus responded ideally, Jesus tells him, *Not far are you from the kingdom of God*. And no one inquired of Him further.

Jesus takes the offensive, asking how the scribes can say that Christ is the Son of David when David called Him Lord. BEWARE OF THE SCRIBES, *who want to walk in robes, and want salutations in the*

Overview of MARK

markets, and front seats in the synagogues. These will be getting more excessive judgment.

Jesus observes the poor widow's offering and notes that she contributed more than any. She gave all that she had; her whole livelihood. Others simply gave out of their excess.

CHAPTER 13

Olivet discourse (13:1)

Jesus tells His disciples the great buildings in Jerusalem will be destroyed. He then speaks of the end times. Many will come in My name and will deceive many. Battles and tidings of battles. Nation roused against nation; kingdom against kingdom. Quakes. Famines and disturbances. This is just the beginning. They shall be giving you up. To all the nations first must be heralded the evangel. Brother will give up brother to death. You will be hated by all because of My name. Yet he who endures to the end shall be saved. When you see the abomination of desolation declared by Daniel the prophet, flee into the mountains. There will be affliction such has not occurred. Except the Lord discounts the days, no flesh at all would be saved. There will be false christs and false prophets, giving signs and miracles. The sun will be darkened; the stars will fall from heaven, and the powers in the heavens will be shaken. And then shall they be seeing the Son of Mankind coming in the clouds with much power and glory.

Learn a parable from the fig tree. When the bough is tender and the leaves sprout, summer is near. *By no means may this generation be passing by until the time when all these things may be occurring.*

> The things Jesus describes *should* have occurred in that generation, but He goes on to warn that no one knows the time. It is a secret that God has not confided to anyone; not even Jesus. Jesus reveals nothing about the delay that has occurred in the past 2000 years; a delay that resulted from Israel's rejection of the kingdom. But that was in fact God's intention, resulting in a far greater grace that benefits all mankind.
>
> The present generation *may* not pass until these things *may* be occurring, but in reality the generation *did* pass. Following Israel's rejection of the kingdom there has been a pause that was not revealed, and was not known to Jesus. And 2000 years later we await the final days of God's plan that will result in the reconciliation of all mankind.

Overview of MARK

No one knows the day or hour; not the messengers nor the Son, but only the Father. *Watch;* for you are not aware when the lord of the house is coming.

CHAPTER 14

Passover (14:1)

As Passover nears, the chief priests and scribes seeks to kill Him. Jesus is anointed by a woman. Judas agrees to betray Him. He celebrates the Passover with the Twelve. He tells of His impending death and resurrection. *After my rousing I shall be preceding you into Galilee.* He predicts Peter's denial.

Gethsemane (14:32)

Judas betrays Him. Jesus is arrested and taken before Caiaphas, the chief priest, who asks, Are you the Christ, the Son of God, the Blessed? Jesus replies: *I am; and you shall be seeing the Son of Mankind sitting at the right hand of power and coming with the clouds of heaven.* The chief priest alleges that Jesus is guilty of *blasphemy* and deserving of death.

> Some say this proves that Jesus has claimed to be God, but a charge of blasphemy does not mean one has claimed to be God the Father. *Blasphemos* in the Greek simply means to "calumniate" or to make false or defamatory statements. If the chief priest felt Jesus was claiming to be the Christ (Messiah) and the *Son* of God, he would view this as a false or defamatory statement and therefore blasphemy. Jesus is not here saying, "I am the same person as God the Father." As a matter of fact, He goes out of His way throughout the gospels to say that He is lesser than God the Father, and simply "commissioned" by God the Father.

Peter denies Jesus.

CHAPTER 15

Trial (15:1)

Jesus appears before Pilate. When given a choice to release one prisoner, the chief priests excite the throng to call for Bar-Abbas to be released and Jesus to be crucified.

Crucifixion (15:16)

As He dies, the curtain of the temple is rent in two, and the centurion observes, Truly, this Man was the Son of God. Joseph from Arimathea,

Overview of MARK

who himself also was anticipating the kingdom of God coming, claims Jesus' body and places Him in a tomb.

> Once again observe the expectation of those who believed Jesus; the kingdom of God coming upon the earth as it is in heaven ... not "going to heaven."

CHAPTER 16

Resurrection ^(16:1)

Mary Magdalene and Mary the mother of James and Salome buy spices and come to the tomb to prepare Jesus' body *early in the morning on one of the Sabbaths.*

> Not "Easter Sunday" morning, but *on one of the Sabbaths.* Remember that Israel observed a weekly Sabbath each Saturday, and every special Feast Day was also considered a Sabbath.

They see a youth clothed in a white robe in the tomb, telling them: He was roused. He is not here. ... Go, say to His disciples and to Peter, that He is preceding you into Galilee.

He had risen *in the morning in the first Sabbath* (16:9) and appeared first to Mary Magdalene. When she reports on His resurrection to others who were coming, they disbelieve. Jesus then manifests Himself in a different form to two who were walking, and when they report to the others they also disbelieve. Jesus is then manifested to the Eleven. He reproaches their unbelief and hardheartedness.

The "Great Commission" ^(16:15)

Jesus says to them: *Go into all the world; herald the evangel to the entire creation. He who believes and is baptized shall be saved, yet he who disbelieves shall be condemned.* He also tells them signs will occur among those who believe. They will cast out demons in His name; they will speak in new languages; they will pick up serpents without being harmed; they will place hands on the sick and they will be healed.

> Observe that this commission is given only to the Eleven. Many today try to replicate these events, yet those with the strongest of faith often die when bitten by the serpent. And, as we will discuss when reviewing Paul's later writings, languages (tongues) will cease and were not intended to be a permanent thing. Also observe that those *condemned* for not believing are not condemned "forever and ever," for Paul will later reveal the consummation at the end of the ages when all are reconciled to God, when

Overview of MARK

all knees are bowed, and when God becomes All in all (1 Corinthians 15). Remember as we read Mark, this is but a step in the process whereby God is working in accord with the counsel of His will to accomplish His desire and plan; the salvation of all. (1 Timothy 2:4)

Ascension. (16:19)

Jesus is taken up into heaven and is seated at the right hand of God. They come away and herald everywhere, and signs follow them.

RECAP

Consider Mark's account of the ministry of Jesus when He walked the earth; a ministry TO ISRAEL and not the Gentile nations or the Body of Christ. All Scripture is inspired (2 Timothy 3:16) but we must observe a pattern of sound words (2 Timothy 1:13) and we must rightly divide the Scriptures. (2 Timothy 2:15)

Mark's account is brief and to the point. Fast paced and action packed. Filled with the connective *immediately* or *straightway* (*eutheos* and *euthus* in the Greek), we see Jesus moving quickly from one scene to the next. He comes into Galilee, enters Capernaum, goes beside the sea, ascends a mountain, enters into the country of Gergesenes, etc.

Mark's account covers many of the same events as Matthew but from a different perspective, for Mark has a different purpose. Matthew portrayed Jesus as CHRIST (*Messiah*) and KING. For this reason we saw the extensive genealogy to prove that Jesus was qualified. And there were many references from Old Testament prophecy to show that Jesus fulfilled these prophecies. But Mark portrays Jesus as a SERVANT; the SON OF MAN. There is no genealogy, as none is needed for his purpose.

According to E. W. Bullinger in *The Companion Bible*, Jesus is addressed as *Lord* 73 times in the other three gospel accounts (37 times by His disciples and 36 times by others). But in Mark He is referred to as *Lord* only 2 times, and in both instances after His resurrection. The focus is on His activities and movements. The word *law* does not occur in Mark, as the focus is on deeds and *service*.

We must remember that the four gospel accounts are not simply four duplicate narratives of the life of Jesus. They were not intended to be "harmonized" as many attempt to do. Each writer has a specific and singular purpose that determined his selection and arrangement of

Overview of MARK

material. Matthew portrays Jesus as *King*, Mark as *Servant*, Luke as *Man* and John as *Son of God*.

Overview of MARK

Luke

An Overview of the Scriptures, by
BOB EVELY © *2018.*
An Independent Minister of Christ Jesus
Of the church at Wilmore, Kentucky

It is assumed that the reader has previously considered the overviews of Matthew of Mark, and we will not repeat many of the same comments in parallel passages.

CHAPTER 1

Why does Luke write? (1:1)

That you may be recognizing the certainty of the words concerning which you were instructed.

> Luke reports that there were many written narratives in circulation concerning Jesus' words and actions. Still, he sees the need to provide his account to Theophilus. Why? Luke saw the need to set the record straight and provide an accurate and legitimate account on which Theophilus could depend.

John the Baptist foretold (1:5)

There is a priest (Zechariah) and his wife (Elizabeth) who are just and blameless before God; living in accord with all the precepts and just statutes. They have no children, as Elizabeth is barren, and they are advanced in age. Gabriel, a *messenger of the Lord*, comes to Zechariah. Gabriel stood before God and was *dispatched* to speak to Zechariah and to bring *this evangel*.

> EVANGEL is most often translated *gospel* and simply means *good news*. Here the good news concerns the coming birth of John the Baptist. *Angel* (*angellos* in the Greek) means *messenger*. In this case the messenger is Gabriel, who has been *dispatched* to bring an *evangel* (good news) to Zechariah. Sometimes *angellos* refers to a human messenger; not always a supernatural messenger ("angel") as in this case.

Elizabeth will bear a son, and his name is to be John. He will be great in the sight of the Lord, and will not drink wine and intoxicant but will be filled with the holy spirit while still in the womb. Many of the *sons*

Overview of LUKE

of Israel shall be turning back to the Lord their God. He is to make ready a people formed for the Lord.

> Observe that John's ministry will be directed TO THE SONS OF ISRAEL and not to those of other nations.

Jesus' birth foretold (1:26)

The messenger Gabriel is again dispatched, this time to a virgin in Nazareth named Miriam (often translated Mary). Mary will conceive and bring forth a Son, and His name is to be Jesus. He will be great, and will be called *Son of the Most High*. The Lord God will be giving Him the throne of David, and He will reign over the house of Jacob for the eons. And of His kingdom there will be no end.

> Will Christ reign forever, or for the eons? He will be the heir to David's throne (remember that David was king of ISRAEL). He will reign *for the eons* (aion in the Greek), not forever as most translations claim. We see in 1 Corinthians 15 that Christ will reign *until* all is subjected to Him, after which He surrenders the throne to God the Father having accomplished the mission assigned to Him. So He will not reign forever, but *until* these things take place. But while Jesus will not reign forever; the kingdom will endure forever. For *of His kingdom there shall be no end.*

The holy spirit will come upon Mary and generate the child Who will be called the Son of God.

> While Mary will be the birth mother, Jesus will be fathered by the holy spirit and will therefore be the Son of God.

Birth of John (1:57)

John is born and is circumcised on the eighth day. Zechariah prophesies, *Blessed be the Lord,* THE GOD OF ISRAEL, *for He visits and makes a redemption* FOR HIS PEOPLE, *and rouses a horn of salvation* FOR US IN THE HOUSE OF DAVID ... *salvation from our enemies.*

Now you also, little boy, a prophet of the Most High shall be called, for you shall be going before in the sight of the Lord to make ready His roads, to give the knowledge of salvation TO HIS PEOPLE *in the pardon of their sin.*

Overview of LUKE

The GOD OF ISRAEL, the HOUSE OF DAVID. Thus far Luke's account is directed ONLY TO ISRAEL and not to those of other nations.

CHAPTER 2

Birth of Jesus (2:1)

Jesus is born in Bethlehem. A messenger of the Lord proclaims to shepherds, *I am bringing you an evangel of great joy which will be for the entire people, for today was brought forth to you a Saviour Who is Christ, the Lord.*

Coming to Jerusalem to be circumcised they are approached by Simeon, who had been apprised by the holy spirit that he would not die until he is acquainted with the Lord's Christ. Simeon observes, My eyes perceived Thy Salvation ... a Light for the revelation of nations, and the Glory of Thy people Israel.

> He is to be the glory of Israel; and also a light for the nations. First Israel; and then, indirectly, the nations. This will be the case until Paul later reveals a new revelation with no preference given to Israel, but with the nations and Israel as joint heirs.

Jesus' childhood (2:39)

They return to Nazareth, and Jesus grows up *staunch in spirit, being filled with wisdom, and the grace of God was on Him*. Every year they go to Jerusalem for the festival of the Passover. At one Passover, when Jesus is twelve years old, He does not return home with His family and is later found in the sanctuary in Jerusalem, seated in the midst of the teachers, hearing them and inquiring of them. All those hearing Him are amazed at His understanding and answers. He progresses *in wisdom and stature, and in favor with God and men.*

> *Sanctuary* comes from the Greek *hiero* which means sacred place. This is a Jewish concept; that a physical place is sacred or holy. Today's churches perpetuate this idea with their sanctuaries and with the notion of their being houses of God. But Jesus will later teach that God does not reside in a specific, physical place. This is an example of carrying a Jewish concept from a previous era, with its Temple and sanctuaries, into the churches of our day.

CHAPTER 3

Overview of LUKE

John's ministry begins (3:1)

In the wilderness John receives a declaration of God. He comes to the area around the Jordan *heralding a baptism of repentance for the pardon of sins.* As written in Isaiah, *The voice of one imploring: In the wilderness make ready the road of the Lord! Straight ... be making the highways of Him. ... All flesh shall see the salvation of God.*

> Verses 1-2 provide some specific historic benchmarks that allow us to know the precise time this occurred; in the fifteenth year of the government of Tiberius Caesar, Pontius Pilate being governor of Judea.

As throngs come to John to be baptized he says, *Progeny of vipers! Who intimates to you to be fleeing from the impending indignation? Produce, then, fruits worthy of repentance.* When they ask what to do, John responds, He who has two tunics, let him be sharing with him who has none, and let him who has food be doing likewise. To the tribute collectors he says, Impose nothing more than has been prescribed to you. To the soldiers, Be intimidating no one, neither be blackmailing, and be sufficed with your rations. When asked if he is the Christ, John answers, In water I am baptizing you. Yet coming is One stronger than I ... He will be baptizing you in holy spirit and fire ... gathering the grain into His barn, yet the chaff shall He burn up with *unextinguished fire.*

When Herod is exposed by John concerning Herodias, his brother's wife, he locks up John in jail.

Jesus is baptized (3:21)

As Jesus is baptized the holy spirit descends on Him and a voice comes out of heaven: *Thou art My Son, the Beloved; in Thee I delight.* At this time Jesus is about thirty years old.

Genealogy (3:23)

> In Appendix 99 of the *Companion Bible*, Mr. Bullinger explains the difference between the genealogies of Matthew and Luke. Matthew's genealogy presents the line from Abraham to Joseph, the earthly father of Jesus. Luke presents the line from Adam to Mary, the mother of Jesus. In the Luke account, Joseph is said to be the son of Heli, (3:23) but this is true only in the legal sense through his marriage to Mary. According to the flesh Joseph is the son of Jacob.

CHAPTER 4

Overview of LUKE

Trial in the wilderness (4:1)
Jesus is led in the spirit in the wilderness for forty days, undergoing trial by the Adversary. When the trials end, the Adversary withdraws from Him until an appointed time.

Teaching in the synagogues (4:14)
Returning to Galilee His fame spreads, and He teaches in their synagogues, being glorified by all.

Jesus publicly declares (4:16)
According to His custom on the day of the sabbaths, He enters the synagogue and stands to read from Isaiah. *The spirit of the Lord is on Me, on account of which He anoints Me to bring the evangel to the poor. He has commissioned Me to heal the crushed heart, to herald to captives a pardon, and to the blind the receiving of sight; to dispatch the oppressed with a pardon, to herald an acceptable year of the Lord.*

As all eyes watch intently He says to them, *Today this scripture is fulfilled in your ears.* All are filled with fury and they cast Him outside the city where they intend to push Him over the precipice. But He passes through their midst.

He teaches in Capernaum and they are astonished at His teaching, for His word was with authority.

Demon cast out (4:33)
The demon cries out, Did you come to destroy us? I am aware who you are – the holy One of God. Jesus rebukes the demon and instructs it to be still, and He casts it out of the man. All observe His authority and power, and *a hubbub* goes out concerning Him throughout the country.

Healings (4:38)
Jesus heals Simon's mother-in-law. All who are infirm with various diseases are led to Him and He cures them. Demons are cast out of many and they say, You are the Christ, the Son of God. But He does not let them speak, *for they had perceived that He is the Christ.*

Jesus' commission (4:42)
To other cities also I must bring the evangel of the kingdom of God, for FOR THIS WAS I COMMISSIONED. *And He was heralding in the synagogues of Judea.*

Jesus was not commissioned by God to bring healing or to perform miracles. These things simply accompanied His heralding, validating His authority. His commission and purpose was to herald the evangel of the coming kingdom.

CHAPTER 5

Peter and others follow (5:1)

Simon had been fishing the entire night but did not catch a single fish. Jesus instructs him to return to the depths and lower the nets for a catch. Peter obeys and catches a multitude of fish. Jesus tells him, *From now on men you shall be catching alive.* Peter and those with him leave all and follow Him.

Healings (5:12)

A leper is healed and Jesus charges him to speak to no one. But the account spreads and vast throngs come to hear and to be healed. Jesus retreats to the wilderness and prays.

A paralytic is brought to Jesus and lowered through the roof. Jesus sees their faith and says to the man, *Pardoned are your sins.* He sees that the Pharisees are reasoning, *Who is this who is speaking blasphemies? Who is able to pardon sins except God only?* Jesus says to them, *That you may be perceiving that the Son of Mankind has authority on earth to pardon sins ... and* He says to the paralytic, *Rouse and pick up your cot and go into your house.* All are amazed and glorify God.

Levi is called (5:27)

Leaving all, Levi follows and hosts a great reception in his house. A vast throng of tribute collectors and others with them come.

Criticism (5:30)

Pharisees and their scribes complain about Jesus eating and drinking with tribute collectors and sinners.

Those who are sound have no need of a physician, but those who have an illness. I have not come to call the just, but sinners, to repentance.

They complain that while John's disciples frequently fast and make petitions, as do the disciples of the Pharisees, Jesus' disciples do not.

You cannot make the sons of the bridal chamber fast while the bridegroom is with them.

Parable of the wineskins (5:36)

If one places a patch from a new cloak onto an old cloak it will tear. And if one puts fresh wine into old wineskins they will burst.

> Jesus is teaching them a new paradigm. The Pharisees see much wrong with Jesus, for they attempt to place Him into the old paradigm; the old wineskins.

CHAPTER 6

More criticism (6:1)

The Pharisees criticize Jesus and His disciples for plucking ears on a Sabbath. But Jesus notes that David once ate showbread that was to be eaten only by the priests. *The Son of Mankind is Lord of the Sabbath.*

Jesus heals a man with a withered hand on the Sabbath, asking them: Is it allowed on the Sabbath to do good or to do evil; to save a soul or to destroy? They begin to consider what they should be doing to Jesus.

Jesus chooses twelve apostles (6:12)

Jesus goes into the mountain and prays throughout the night. From His disciples He chooses twelve whom He names apostles.

> The Greek for apostle is *apostellos* which means commission. An apostle is one who has received a commission.

A vast multitude from Judea, Jerusalem and maritime Tyre and Sidon come to hear Him and to be healed, and He healed all.

Beatitudes & Sermon on the Mount (6:20)

Here we find a less complete version of the Beatitudes and Sermon on the Mount than Matthew's account. (Matthew 5:3)

- ✓ Love your enemies (6:27)
- ✓ Do unto men as you are wanting them to do to you (6:31)
- ✓ Love your enemies and be doing good, expecting nothing in return, and your wages will be vast in the heavens (6:35)
- ✓ Be not judging, and under no circumstances may you be judged (6:37)
- ✓ Give, and it shall be given to you (6:38)
- ✓ The blind cannot guide the blind, and a disciple is not above his teacher (6:39)
- ✓ Why observe the mote in your brother's eye, having a beam in your own eye? (6:41)
- ✓ A tree is known by its fruit (6:43)
- ✓ The good man out of the good treasure of his heart is bringing forth that which is good (6:45)

Overview of LUKE

✓ Why call me Lord and not do what I am saying? The one who hears My words and is doing them is like a man building a house with its foundation on a rock (6:46)

> Remember that Jesus is directing His message to Israel, to prepare them for entrance into the kingdom once it is restored upon the earth. Much of what He says will have literal application in daily life within the kingdom. While the Body of Christ today can understand the Lord's heart through these words, we must be careful not to enforce a literal application within the Body of Christ today. We are not looking for the kingdom to be restored upon the earth. We are looking for the Lord to come and call us into the heavenly realms where we will serve Him there in the eons to come. We must be careful not to become legalistic while upon the earth in this present wicked eon, interpreting these words of Jesus as being written directly to us in our present day.

CHAPTER 7

Healings (7:1)

In Capernaum, Jesus heals the slave of a centurion who is about to die. The centurion, who loved Israel and had built the synagogue, does not want to inconvenience Jesus. He asks Jesus to simply say the word and his boy would be healed; just as a man having authority can command his soldiers. Jesus replies, Not even in Israel did I find so much faith. He heals the man's slave.

In the city of Nain, Jesus raises from the dead a widow's son. Those observing fear and glorify God, saying: A great prophet was roused among us! ... God visits His people. Word spreads in the whole of Judea and the country about.

John's inquiry (7:18)

John sends his disciples to ask of Jesus, Art Thou the coming One, or may we be hoping for a different One. Jesus replies, *Report to John what you perceived and hear: that the blind are receiving sight, the lame are walking, lepers are being cleansed, and the deaf are hearing, the dead are being roused, and to the poor the evangel is being brought.*

After John's disciples leave, Jesus speaks to the throngs about John. He is *exceedingly more than a prophet. This is he concerning whom it is written, Lo! I am dispatching My messenger before Thy face, who shall be constructing Thy road in front of Thee.* Jesus tells them there is no

Overview of LUKE

greater prophet than John of those born of women. Yet the smaller, in the kingdom of God is greater than he.

Hearing this, the people; even the tribute collectors; are baptized with the baptism of John. But the Pharisees and those learned in the law repudiate the counsel of God and are not baptized.

> REJECTION! Despite Jesus demonstrating His authority through healings and casting out demons, the leaders of Israel continue to criticize and reject Him.

Invited to the home of a Pharisee (7:36)

Inside a Pharisee's home Jesus is approached by a woman who is a sinner, and she washes and kisses His feet. The Pharisee wonders to himself what manner of prophet Jesus is, as He should know the kind of woman this is. Jesus discerns what he is thinking and tells the man a story of two debtors. One owes 500 denarii and the other owes 50. The creditor forgives both debts. Which of them will be loving him more? Jesus then says to the woman, Pardoned are your sins; for she had loved Him much. Those observing talk among themselves: Who is this who is pardoning sins?

CHAPTER 8

Heralding the evangel (8:1)

Jesus goes city by city and village by village, *heralding and bringing the evangel of the kingdom of God.*

Parable of the sower (8:4)

The seed that is scattered upon good earth produces much fruit. His disciples ask the meaning of the parable and He replies, *To you has it been given to know* THE SECRETS OF THE KINGDOM OF GOD, *yet to the rest in parables, that, observing, they may not be observing, and hearing, they may not be understanding.*

He then explains the parable. The seed is the word of God. Much of the seed is thwarted by the Adversary, by seasons of trial, by worries and riches, and by the gratifications of life. But the seed that is received by a heart that is ideal and good matures and bears fruit.

> The leaders among Israel are rejecting Jesus and His message concerning the kingdom. He will therefore speak only in parables that will not be understood by those who reject Him. But these parables will

Overview of LUKE

reveal the secrets of the kingdom of God to those to whom it is given to understand.

Parable of the lamp (8:16)

No one lights a lamp and then covers it. Nothing is hidden which shall not become apparent. Beware, then, how you are hearing! For whoever may have, to him shall be given, and whoever may not have, from him shall be taken away also what he is supposed to have.

Jesus' mother and brothers (8:19)

When Jesus is told that His mother and brothers are waiting to see Him, He replies, My mother and My brethren are these who are hearing the word of God and doing it.

> Certainly Jesus is not disowning His mother and brothers, but He uses this opportunity to teach an insight using hyperbole (intentional exaggeration). What matters is the hearing and doing of the word of God.

He calms the sea (8:22)

The disciples are frightened, thinking they will perish. They rouse Jesus and He rebukes the wind and calms the sea. He says to them, Where is your faith? And they say to one another, Who is this that can still the winds and calm the waters?

Demons cast into hogs (8:26)

In Gergesenes, Jesus encounters a man who has demons and is living in the tombs. The man cries out, Jesus, Son of God Most High! I beseech Thee, Thou shouldst not be tormenting me. The many demons entreat Jesus not to send them into *the submerged chaos*, but instead allow them to enter a herd of hogs. Jesus permits this, and when the demons come out of the man and enter the hogs, they run into the lake and perish. When the graziers come they find the man sane. But when they hear the report of how he had been saved, the entire multitude of the surrounding country ask Jesus to leave, *for they were pressed by a great fear*. Jesus tells the man to return home and relate how much God does for him.

Healings (8:40)

Jairus, chief of the synagogue, asks Jesus to come as his daughter has died. Along the way a woman with a hemorrhage for twelve years touches Jesus' cloak and is healed. Jesus knows He has been touched as He feels the power come out from Him. The woman comes trembling and reports before the entire people why she had touched Him and was healed. Jesus says to her: *Your faith has saved you! Go in peace!*

They arrive at Jairus' house and find that his daughter is dead. He says to them, *Fear not; only believe, and she shall be saved.* In the girl's presence He tells them, *Be not lamenting, for she did not die, but is drowsing.* They ridicule Jesus, knowing that the girl had died, and He casts them outside. He rouses the girl *and back turns her spirit, and she rose instantly.* He tells them to tell no one about this.

CHAPTER 9

Commissioning of the Twelve (9:1)

Jesus gives power and authority to the Twelve over demons and to cure diseases. *He commissions them to be heralding the kingdom of God and to be healing the infirm.* If they should not be receiving you, come out of that city.

They pass through the villages, bringing the evangel and curing everywhere. Herod hears of these events and asks Who this is about whom he is hearing such things? He seeks to become acquainted with Him.

Returning, the apostles tell Jesus all that they did and taught. He retreats privately to Bethsaida. The throngs follow and He welcomes them, speaking to them concerning the kingdom of God. Those having need of a cure He heals.

Feeding the 5000 (9:12)

With only five cakes of bread and two fishes, about 5000 men are fed.

Who do you say that I am? (9:18)

The throngs are saying that Jesus is John the Baptist, or Elijah, or a prophet of the ancients that arose. But Jesus asks the apostles, Who are *you* saying that I am? Peter replies, The Christ of God. And Jesus warns them to tell no one. *The Son of Mankind must be suffering much, and be rejected by the elders and chief priests and scribes, and be killed, and the third day be roused.*

On following (9:23)

If any are to follow let him disown himself and pick up his cross daily and follow Me. Whosoever may be wanting to save his soul shall be

Overview of LUKE

destroying it, yet whoever should be destroying his soul on My account, he shall be *saving* it. For what does a man benefit, gaining the whole world, yet destroying or forfeiting himself?

Whoever may be ashamed of Me, the Son of Mankind shall be ashamed when He comes in the glory of Him, and of the Father and of the holy messengers. And some standing here will under no circumstances be tasting death till they should be perceiving the kingdom of God.

The Transfiguration (9:28)

Peter, John and James accompany Jesus as He ascends into the mountain to pray. Jesus' face becomes different and His garments glitter white. Two men talk with Him; Moses and Elijah. They speak of His *exodus* that is about to occur in Jerusalem.

Peter suggests that they make three tabernacles for them. Just then a cloud overshadows them and a voice comes out of the cloud: *This is My Son, the Chosen; Him be hearing.* And at that moment Jesus stand alone. They tell no one what they had seen.

Demon cast out (9:37)

A man asks Jesus to see his son, for His disciples have been unable to cast a demon from him. *O generation unbelieving and perverse! Till when shall I be with you and bear with you?* He rebukes the unclean spirit and *heals* the boy. Jesus tells His disciples, *Be laying up these sayings in your ears, for the Son of Mankind is about to be given up into the hands of men.* But they were ignorant of what He was saying; IT WAS SCREENED FROM THEM *that they may not be sensing it.*

> The disciples are ignorant of what He is saying because it was <u>screened</u> from them. It is not God's will that they understand at this point. God's timing!

Who will be greatest? (9:46)

The apostles reason among themselves as to which should be greatest. Jesus tells them, Whosoever should be receiving this little child in My name is receiving Me, and whosoever should be receiving Me is receiving Him who commissions Me. For the one inherently smaller among you all, he is great.

A non-follower is casting out demons in His name (9:49)

The apostles forbid him, for he is not following with them. Jesus tells them, Be not forbidding, for he who is not against you is for you.

Travelling toward Jerusalem (9:51)

They enter a village of the Samaritans to make ready for Him. But they do not receive Him, for He was going to Jerusalem. James and John propose that Jesus bring fire from heaven to consume them, but He rebukes them. And on they go to a different village.

On following (9:57)

Someone proposes that they will follow Jesus wherever He goes. Jesus observes, The jackals have burrows and the flying creatures of heaven roost, yet the Son of Mankind has nowhere that He may be reclining His head.

Jesus says, *Follow Me.* But one wanted first to go and entomb his father. *Let the dead entomb their own dead. Yet you, coming away,* PUBLISH THE KINGDOM OF GOD. Another wanted first to take leave of those in their home. *No one, putting forth his hand on a plow and looking behind, is fit in the kingdom of God.*

> The most important task for Jesus' disciples in that era, consistent with His own commission, is TO PUBLISH THE KINGDOM OF GOD.

CHAPTER 10

Commissioning seventy two disciples (10:1)

He dispatches them two by two into every city and place where He is about to enter, saying, The harvest is vast, yet the workers are few. Beseech, then, the Lord of the harvest. ... I am dispatching you as lambs in the midst of wolves.

If received they are to remain, curing the infirm and proclaiming, *Near to you is the kingdom of God.* And if they are not received they are to come into the square and say, *Near to you is the kingdom of God!*

It will be more tolerable for Sodom in that day than for that city. To Chorazin and Bethsaida they would proclaim, *If the powerful deeds which are occurring in you occurred in Tyre and Sidon, long ago they would repent ... For Tyre and Sidon will it be more tolerable in the judging than for you.* And to Capernaum: *Not to heaven shall you be exalted! To the unseen shall you subside.*

> The purpose of the *powerful deeds* was to demonstrate the nearness of the kingdom and to gain repentance. But this is not occurring; the kingdom is being rejected. Also observe that those in Tyre and Sidon would have repented had they been fortunate enough to see such powerful deeds. Why, then, were they not given powerful deeds? If, ultimately, those of Tyre and Sidon are cast into eternal torment this would be a demonstration of injustice on God's part. But if those of Tyre and Sidon, like all mankind, are ultimately reconciled and saved; their history, and this current rejection by Israel in Jesus' day, become a part of God's unfolding plan. What we see here is a work in progress.

Afterwards the seventy two return with joy, reporting that the demons were subject to them in His name. *I have given you authority to be treading upon serpents and scorpions and over the entire power of the enemy, and nothing shall be injuring you. But do not rejoice that the spirits are subject to you; rejoice that your names are engraved in the heavens.*

Jesus acclaims the Father, *for Thou dost conceal these things from the wise and intelligent and Thou dost reveal them to minors.* To the disciples He says, *All was given up to Me by My Father, and no one knows who the Son is except the Father, and who the Father is except the Son, and* WHOMSOEVER THE SON MAY BE INTENDING TO UNVEIL HIM.

> It is not a matter of being more intelligent or commendable in recognizing and accepting the Lord and the kingdom. Those who understand and receive Him are those to whom He unveils Himself. But why does He not simply unveil Himself to all? Could it be that those who reject Him in these days are playing a necessary part in God's plan to ultimately save all? Much like Joseph's brothers who meant their deeds to harm Joseph, when in fact all that happened to Joseph was God's intent in order to carry out His ultimate plan?

Parable of the Good Samaritan (10:27)

A lawyer asks what he must do to enjoy *the allotment of life eonian.* Jesus asks the man what is written in the law? *You shall be loving the Lord your God out of your whole heart, and with your whole soul, and with your whole strength, and with your whole comprehension, and your associate as yourself.* Jesus acknowledges this is correct. *This be doing and you shall be living.* When the man asks, *who is my associate?*

Jesus replies with the parable of the good Samaritan. He tells the man that like the one doing the merciful thing in the parable, *Go and do likewise*.

> Unlike the *faith alone* message Paul proclaims to the Body of Christ in a later era, here we see that entrance into the kingdom and the resulting *allotment of life eonian* has to do with good works. We must be careful to *rightly divide* the word of God, properly applying that which pertains to us in our present era without mixing Paul's evangel to us with the evangel of the kingdom being proclaimed to Israel by Jesus. That message was for a different people-group in a different era. If we mix evangels, we become as those Paul addressed in Galatians.

Martha and Mary (10:38)

As Jesus visits, Martha is distracted with serving. She complains that her sister has left her to serve alone. *You are worrying and in a tumult about many things, but of these things there is need of few if any*. Mary chooses the good part which will not be wrested from her.

CHAPTER 11

The "Lord's Prayer" (11:1)

The disciples ask, *Lord teach us to pray*. He responds with what is commonly called "The Lord's Prayer." Note especially the words, *Thy kingdom come. Thy will be done, as in heaven, on earth also.*

> The kingdom is near. It will one day come upon the earth (see Revelation), and the earth will see God's will accomplished as is currently the case in heaven. But not yet! God's timing!

Parables on prayer (11:5)

If one asks for bread but his friend is in bed, even if the friend will not rise because of friendship surely he will rise *because of his pestering*.

Request, and it shall be given to you. Seek, and you shall find. Knock, and it shall be opened to you. For everyone who is requesting is obtaining and who is seeking is finding, and to the one knocking it shall be opened.

If a son asks for bread, his father will not give him a stone. If he asks for fish his father will not give him a serpent. If he asks for an egg his father will not give him a scorpion. *If you, then, being inherently wicked, are aware how to give good gifts to your children, how much rather will the Father Who is out of heaven, be giving holy spirit to those requesting Him!*

> Observe that man is inherently wicked, not inherently good. So much for the devices of men apart from God's righteousness and goodness.

Demon cast out (11:14)

Some claim He casts out demons by Beelzeboul, the chief of demons. But *how can Satan be casting out Satan? ... Every kingdom divided against itself is being desolated, and house against house is falling. ... If I, by the finger of God, am casting out demons, consequently the kingdom of God outstrips in time to you.*

He offers an analogy. As Satan guards his possessions he is conquered by one stronger, who takes away his armor and distributes his spoils. *He who is not with Me is against Me, and he who is not gathering with Me is scattering.*

If an unclean spirit leaves and finds no rest, it will return. And if the home it left is unoccupied, the spirit will return, bringing seven others who are more wicked.

Hearing and doing the word of God (11:27)

A woman praises Him: Happy the womb that bears Thee. But He responds, *Happy are those who are hearing the word of God and maintaining it.*

> Repeatedly Jesus is telling His audience; the important thing is HEARING the *evangel* ... the word of God ... and DOING it. Faith plus works!

Wicked generation seeks a sign (11:29)

This generation is a *wicked generation*. A sign it is seeking, and a sign shall not be given to it except the sign of Jonah. The queen of the south came from the ends of the earth to hear the wisdom of Solomon, and more than Solomon is here. The Ninevites repented at Jonah's heralding, and more than Jonah is here.

No one hides a lamp (11:33)

A lamp is placed on a lampstand so those coming and going can see it. The eye is the body's lamp. If your eye is *single*, your whole body is lighted.

Overview of LUKE

> Be careful little eyes what you see!

Woe to the Pharisees (11:37)

He lunches with the Pharisees and they note that he is not first *baptized* before eating.

> From this context we note that the Greek word for *baptize* simply means wash; thereby shedding light on the intended significance on the act of baptism.

Pharisees are cleansing the outside of the cup and the platter, yet your inside is brimming with rapacity and wickedness.

Woe to you, Pharisees, for taking tithes while forgoing judging and the love of God. You love the front seats in the synagogues and the salutations in the markets. Hypocrites!

Woe to you who are learned in the law, and who are loading men with loads that are hard to bear, while you yourselves are not lifting loads. You build tombs for the prophets, yet your fathers killed them.

Woe to you who are learned in the law, for you take away the key of knowledge. You do not enter, and you prevent others from entering.

After hearing these things the Pharisees quiz him further, trying to ambush Him and pounce on something He says, so as to accuse Him.

CHAPTER 12

Beware of the Pharisees (12:1)

He turns to His disciples: *Take heed of the leaven of the Pharisees which is hypocrisy. Nothing is covered up which shall not be revealed.*

Don't fear the one who kills the body and who can do nothing more. Fear Him Who, after killing, has authority to be casting into Gehenna.

Yet, do not fear. Not one sparrow is forgotten in God's sight. Even the hairs of your head have all been numbered.

The unpardoned sin (12:8)

Everyone avowing Me in front of men, I will avow in front of the messengers of God. But he who disowns Me before men, I will renounce before the messengers of God.

Everyone who declares a word against the Son of Mankind will be pardoned, but the one who blasphemes against the holy spirit shall not be pardoned.

Overview of LUKE

When you are brought before the authorities, do not fear what you should say. The holy spirit will be teaching you in the same hour.

Guard against greed (12:13)

Guard against all greed, for one's life is not in the superfluity of his possessions. He tells them a parable concerning a rich man who builds larger barns to gather all his grain, and who thinks: Rest, eat, drink and make merry. *Imprudent one! In this night your soul are they demanding from you. ... Thus is he who is hoarding for himself and is not rich for God.*

Do not worry (12:22)

Don't worry about the soul, what you may be eating ... or your body, what you should be wearing. Of how much more consequences are you than the flying creatures. And by worrying, who can add to his stature one cubit? The nations worry about what they eat or drink, but your Father is aware that you need these. Be seeking the kingdom of God, and all these things will be added to you.

> Observe the distinction between Israel, which Jesus addresses, and the nations. Israel is given earthly promises and is anticipating an earthly kingdom with Jesus on the throne. The nations would only be blessed indirectly through Israel. In our present day, we within the Body of Christ are not promised earthly blessings ... but spiritual blessings.

Don't fear, for it delights your Father to give you the kingdom. Sell your possessions and give alms. Gain a treasure that cannot be lost to a thief, and that moths cannot decay. Wherever your treasure is, there will your heart be also.

Be watchful (12:35)

Gird your loins and let your lamps be burning. Be like men anticipating their lord, that when he knocks you should immediately open to him. Happy are those the Lord will find *watching*.

Be ready, for the Son of Mankind is coming in an hour which you are not supposing. If a slave should think, My lord is delaying his coming, and should beat his servants and be drunk ... his lord will arrive on a day for which he is not hoping, and shall cut him asunder and appoint his part with the unfaithful.

Overview of LUKE

The slave who knows the will of his lord and does not make ready will receive many lashes. He who does not know the will of his lord will receive few lashes. To whom much was given, from him much will be sought.

I come to bring division, not peace (12:49)
Are you supposing I came to give peace to the earth? No; I came to bring division; father against sons and son against father. When you see a cloud rising in the west, a rainstorm is coming. Hypocrites. The aspect of the sky and the earth you know how to test, yet this era you do not know how to test.

Justice required (12:57)
Why are you not deciding what is just? Take action to be cleared from another, lest he drags you to the judge and you are cast into jail. You will not get out until you pay the last mite.

CHAPTER 13

All (within Israel) must repent (13:1)
Are the Galileans persecuted by Pilate worse sinners than all other Galileans? Were those upon whom the tower in Siloam fell worse than all who live in Jerusalem? No! If you do not repent, all of you will similarly perish.

Parable of the fig tree (13:6)
A man had a fig tree, and for three years he sought fruit but did not find any. Hew it down, then. But the vineyardist replied, Lord, leave it this year also and I will dig and cast manure about it. And if it does not produce fruit in the coming year, then you can hew it down.

> In the interim evil will exist alongside good. The separation will occur when the harvest is ready, in accord with God's timing.

Healing on the sabbath (13:10)
A woman who had been ill and unable to walk upright for eighteen years is healed by Jesus. The chief of the synagogue resents that Jesus cured her on the Sabbath. He replies, Hypocrites! Each of you looses his ox or ass from the manger and gives it drink. Satan binds this woman for eighteen years; must she not be loosed from this bond on the Sabbath day?

Overview of LUKE

Parables of the kingdom of God (13:13)
The kingdom of God is like a mustard seed. It grows and becomes a great tree. The kingdom of God is like leaven, which leavens the whole.

Teaching on entering the kingdom on the way to Jerusalem (13:22)
Are few being saved? Struggle to enter through the *cramped* door. Many will seek to enter and will not be strong enough.

When you stand outside and knock, the householder will say he is not acquainted with you. Withdraw from me, all workers of injustice. There will be lamentation and gnashing of teeth when you see Abraham and Isaac and Jacob and all the prophets in the kingdom of God, yet you are *cast outside*.

They will be arriving from east and west and from north and south and will be made to recline in the kingdom of God. They are last who will be first, and they are first who will be last.

> The Pharisees will find that they will be prevented from entering the kingdom when it is established upon the earth, while those whom they least expect from east and west, north and south among the nations will enter.

Jesus warned of Herod by some Pharisees (13:31)
I am casting out demons and performing healings today and tomorrow, and on the third day I am being *perfected*. Moreover, it is not credible that a prophet perish outside of Jerusalem.

Jerusalem; how many times do I wish to assemble your children, but you will not. By no means may you be perceiving Me till the time will be arriving when you should be saying, Blessed is He Who is coming in the name of the Lord.

CHAPTER 14

Healing on the sabbath (14:1)
He enters the house of one of the chiefs of the Pharisees and is approached by a man who needs healing. After healing the man He asks, Whose son or ox of yours will be falling into a well and he will not immediately pull him up on the sabbath day?

Parable: Taking the best seats (14:7)
At wedding festivities, don't occupy the first places, lest one held in higher honor comes and you are asked to move. With shame you will go

to the last place. Instead, occupy the last place. The host may come and ask you to move forward, and glory will be yours. Everyone exalting himself shall be humbled, and the one humbling himself shall be exalted.

When you host a reception, invite the poor, the cripples, the lame and the blind. They have nothing to repay you, and it will be repaid you in the resurrection of the just.

Parable of the great dinner (14:15)

A man prepares a great dinner and invites many. He sends his slave to go to those invited, but they make excuses. When the slave reports back, the householder says, Go into the squares and streets of the city, and lead in here the poor, and cripples, and blind, and lame. After doing so there is still more room and the lord instructs, Come out into the roads and stone dikes, and compel them to enter, that my house may be crammed. And not one of those men who are invited shall be tasting of my dinner.

> Who will attend the great dinner? This is a story to illustrate the coming kingdom. And again Jesus is pointing out that the Pharisees will be excluded, and unexpected guests will take their place ... those the Pharisees would least expect to be there.

The difficulty of following (14:25)

Anyone who is coming and not hating his father and mother and wife and children and brothers and sisters, and still more his soul, he cannot be My disciple. Anyone who is coming and not bearing his cross cannot be My disciple.

> Hating father and mother? Jesus uses hyperbole to show the importance of following. Certainly He does not advocate literally *hating* father and mother, which would be inconsistent with His teachings concerning love and forgiveness. But He is teaching that following, and the things of God, are the most important things to consider.

Who would attempt to build a tower without first calculating its cost to see if he has the ability? What king would go to battle without first determining if he can be successful? Anyone who is not parting with all of his possessions cannot be My disciple.

CHAPTER 15

Overview of LUKE

Parable of the lost sheep and the lost coin (15:1)
The Pharisees and scribes complain when Jesus eats with sinners. He shares a parable about a man having a hundred sheep. When the man loses one, he leaves behind the ninety-nine and goes after the lost one until he finds it. Similarly if a woman has ten drachmas and loses one, she searches the entire house until she finds it.

Parable of the Prodigal Son (15:11)
A man had two sons. The younger asks his father for his part of the estate and then travels to a far country and lives recklessly, spending it all. When he returns his father welcomes him and calls for a calf to be sacrificed for a dinner, *for this my son was dead and revives; he was lost and was found.* When the elder son objects, his father replies: *You are always with me, and all mine is yours. Yet we must be merry and rejoice, seeing that this your brother was dead and revives, and was lost and was found.*

CHAPTER 16

Parable of the unjust administrator (16:1)
A rich man has an administrator who is accused of wasting his possessions. The administrator is asked to give an account. He takes steps so that when he is deposed from his administration he will be received by those having accounts. He calls each of the debtors and offers to settle for a portion of the debt if they pay quickly. The lord applauds the unjust administrator for acting prudently, for the *sons of this eon* are more prudent, above the sons of light in their own generation.

Jesus asks His disciples, Am I saying to make friends with the mammon of injustice so when it defaults they will receive you in the eonian tabernacles? *He who is faithful in the least is faithful in much also, and he who is unjust in the least is unjust in much also. ... No domestic can be slaving for two lords, for either he will be hating one and loving the other, or he will be upholding one and despising the other. You cannot slave for God and mammon.*

He says to the Pharisees who are inherently fond of money, You are justifying yourselves in the sight of men, yet God knows your hearts, for what is high among men is an abomination in the sight of God.

Overview of LUKE

The kingdom of God is being bought, and everyone is *violently forcing into it,* and the violent are snatching it. But it is easier for heaven and earth to pass by than for one serif of the law to fall.

> The Pharisees believe that as sons of Abraham they are automatically qualified to enter the kingdom. They ignore the means God has put into place, and they attempt to *violently force* themselves into the kingdom.

Adultery (16:18)

One who dismisses his wife and marries another commits adultery. And one who marries the woman dismissed from her husband commits adultery.

The rich man and Lazarus (16:19)

A poor man (Lazarus) and a rich man both die. The rich man, in torment, sees Abraham from afar and Lazarus with him. He asks Abraham to be merciful to him, but is reminded that he received his good things in his lifetime while Lazarus received evil things. The rich man is not able to cross the great chasm between them. He asks that at least Lazarus be sent to warn his brothers so they do not also come to *this place of torment,* but Abraham replies: If they do not hear Moses and the prophets, neither will they be persuaded if someone should rise from among the dead.

> This account is found only in Luke. Confusion and misunderstanding occur when one attempts to literalize a portion of Scripture that is figurative. The story of the rich man and Lazarus is clearly a <u>figurative</u> teaching about stewardship that started in 15:1 with the parables of the lost sheep, the lost coin and the prodigal son.
>
> Some try to use this portion of Scripture as proof of the state of wicked sinners after death. They are conscious, engulfed in flames and in extreme torment for all eternity. But let's make a few observations.
>
> 1. Some say the rich man & Lazarus is not a parable because Jesus did not specifically identify it as a parable. But Jesus also did not say that the stories of the lost coin, the prodigal or the unjust steward are parables; yet most will agree they are. Consider the context. The rich man is one more in a series of parables in Luke 15-16.
>
> 2. Many teachers in the day who spoke in Semitic environments often used symbolism and parables. Often incidents are greatly

exaggerated to amplify the teaching. Consider the mustard seed which does not literally grow into the largest of trees. (Matthew 13:32) And when Paul suggests one heap coals of fire onto the head of one's enemy, was this to be taken literally? (Romans 12:20)

3. Jesus Himself reached the point in His ministry that when talking with the masses He spoke only in parables. (Matthew 13:34-35)

4. Lazarus ate crumbs that fell from the rich man's table. If this is to be taken literally, would Lazarus have eaten enough to survive?

5. When Lazarus went to reside in Abraham's bosom; the breast portion of his body ... is this to be taken literally?

6. If there was a large chasm between Abraham/Lazarus and the rich man, how were they able to talk with one another?

7. If Abraham and Lazarus are in heaven (as many claim), the redeemed would be in constant contact with the sinners being tormented in hell. Seeing the tortured persons writhing in pain, close enough to converse, how can the redeemed find enjoyment in their eternal state? One's unredeemed father, mother, spouse, child would also be suffering in plain view.

8. Does the rich man ask Lazarus to drag him out of the fire? No; but only to place a drop of cold water on his tongue. This would not relieve his pain in the slightest, so what is the point?

9. Lazarus is a transliteration of the Hebrew Eleazar. He is probably a Gentile proselyte, for the image "desiring to be fed with the crumbs which fell from the rich man's table" was typical of Gentile identification. (Matthew 15:22-28)

10. There is one Eleazar in the Scriptures who was associated with Abraham and who seems to fit the theme of the Lord's teaching concerning stewardship. (Genesis 15:2-3) Eleazar is the chief steward of Abraham, and a very faithful steward. He carries out Abraham's command even though it meant the loss of his own inheritance. He thus becomes a "beggar" who possessed nothing of earthly value.

11. Who is the rich man? If the story is taken at face value, and if one believes it teaches things concerning one's eternal destiny in heaven or hell, consider this. Salvation would have nothing to do with faith

or righteousness. Nothing is said of the rich man's character. He is not said to be wicked, dishonest, unjust or immoral. He is simply rich. Nor do we learn much of Lazarus. He is poor, but we are not told that he is righteous or good. Therefore one's eternal destiny, if this is what the story is about, is dependent upon being rich and enjoying the present life, or being poor and not enjoying the present life.

12. This is not simply any rich man. He calls Abraham his father. He is a legal possessor of Abraham's inheritance. He enjoyed the physical blessings given to Abraham's seed. He wore purple. Why would Jesus bother to say anything about the rich man's clothes? Purple is the symbol of kingship; and linen, the symbol of priesthood. In this story the rich man, clearly representative of Israel, is unfaithful with his responsibilities.

13. The great chasm would seem to be similar to that which prevented Moses from entering the promised land, because of his rebellion. Likewise will the rebellious of Israel fail to enter the kingdom when it is established upon the earth.

14. Those charged with being stewards (the leaders of Israel) are not faithful, and their inheritance is forfeited. Those despised by the leaders of Israel (tribute collectors and sinners) are given the inheritance in their place.

15. For any that would use this parable to derive the idea that the dead are alive in a conscious state, this would be in direct contradiction to many other passages that clearly teach the dead know nothing and are in an unconscious sleep state, awaiting the resurrection. (Ecclesiastes 9:5)

16. For any who would believe the rich man & Lazarus is a teaching concerning heaven and hell, consider that Moses never taught anything about going to either heaven or hell. God only promises thru Moses good and bad things here on earth, which is why Israel's expectation was for a Messiah to come and free them from bondage. The Old Testament says nothing at all about one's reward being in heaven, or one's punishment being to burn in hell.

CHAPTER 17

Overview of LUKE

Don't be a snare (17:1)
Woe to him through whom snares are coming. It would be better that a millstone were around his neck and he be cast into the sea than he should be snaring one of these little ones.

Forgive (17:3)
If your brother should be sinning, rebuke him. If he repents, forgive him. If he should be sinning against you seven times a day and turns about and repents seven times a day, forgive him.

Faith as a mustard seed (17:5)
If you have faith as a mustard seed, you would tell this black mulberry to be uprooted and be planted in the sea, and it would obey you.

Slaves, do what is prescribed (17:7)
Does a slave get no thanks when he does what is prescribed? When you are doing things that are prescribed you, be saying: Useless slaves are we. What we ought to do we have done.

Ten lepers are healed (17:1)
Only one of them (a Samaritan) returns, glorifying God and thanking Jesus. Are not the ten cleansed? Yet where are the nine? Did none return to give glory to God except this foreigner?

> It is the unexpected one; the non-Israelite; who gives thanks and glorifies God.

Pharisees ask when the kingdom of God is coming (17:20)
The kingdom of God is not coming with scrutiny. Nor shall they be declaring look here or look there, for the kingdom of God is inside of you.

> It is inside of them to the extent that they receive or reject. And if they receive they begin to live with the expectation of the kingdom's coming, and are empowered by that expectation. But this is not to say that the kingdom is not literally COMING when Christ returns, as we see Jesus describing in the passages immediately following.

Yet to His disciples He says ... (17:22)
Coming is the time when you will long to see the days of the Son of Mankind, and you will not see it. They will declare to you, look there or

look here, but AS THE LIGHTNING FLASHES ACROSS THE SKY THUS WILL BE THE SON OF MANKIND IN HIS DAY.

> His return will be unmistakable. Before that day many will declare that He has come, pointing to certain signs or events to back their claim. But even the destruction of the temple in AD 70 is not "as lightning flashing across the sky." The world continues to await His return.

Signs of the end times (17:25)

But first He must suffer many things and be rejected by this generation. It will be as in the days of Noah; they ate, drank and married until the day Noah entered the ark and the deluge came destroying them all. It will be as in the days of Lot; they ate, drank, bought, sold, planted and built until the day that Lot came out of Sodom, and fire and sulpher rained from heaven and destroyed them all. So will it be on the day the Son of Mankind is unveiled.

There will be two on one couch; one will be taken and the other left. There will be two grinding at the same place; one will be taken and the other left.

CHAPTER 18

Parable of the persistent widow (18:1)

He tells them a parable *that they must always be praying and not despondent*. A widow comes to a judge asking to be avenged from her plaintiff, but for a time he will not grant her request. But later, because of the weariness the widow causes him, he accommodates her request. Should not God be avenging His chosen ones who are imploring Him day and night? At the coming of the Son of Mankind will He be finding faith on the earth?

Parable: Prayer of the Pharisee and the tribute collector (18:9)

A Pharisee and a tribute collector go into the sanctuary to pray. The Pharisee thanks God that he is not like the rest of men: rapacious, unjust, adulterers, or even as the tribute collector. The tribute collector does not even lift his eyes to heaven, but asks God to make a propitiatory shelter for him, a sinner. This man returned home *justified*. Everyone who is exalting himself shall be humbled, yet he who is humbling himself shall be exalted.

Let the children come to Me (18:15)
Do not forbid them, for of such is the kingdom of God. Whoever should not be receiving the kingdom of God as a little child, may under no circumstances be entering into it.

The rich man asks how to enjoy life eonian (18:18)
You are acquainted with the precepts: You should not be committing adultery. You should not be murdering. You should not be stealing. You should not be testifying falsely. Be honoring your father and your mother. The man replies, All of these I maintain from my youth.

Still one thing you lack. Sell whatever you have and distribute to the poor, and you will be having treasure in the heavens. Follow Me. But the man was sorrowful, for he was very rich.

How squeamishly shall those having money be entering into the kingdom of God. For it is easier for a camel to be entering through the eye of a needle than for a rich man to be entering into the kingdom of God.

Those hearing this ask who, then, can be saved? *What is impossible with men is possible with God.*

Making sacrifices for the kingdom (18:28)
Those who leaves house, wife, brothers, parents or children on account of the kingdom of God will be getting back manifold in this era; and *life eonian in the coming eon.*

Jesus predicts His suffering and death (18:31)
The Son of Mankind will be given up to the *nations* and will be scoffed at and outraged and spat upon. They will scourge Him and kill Him. And the third day He will be rising. The twelve understand none of these things; this declaration was HID FROM THEM and they knew not what was said.

Blind man healed (18:35)
The man pleads: Jesus, Son of David, be merciful to me. *Receive sight. Your faith has saved you.*

CHAPTER 19

Zaccheus (19:1)
Zaccheus, a chief tribute collector who is rich, climbs a tree so as to see Jesus. Zaccheus! Hurry! Descend, for today I must remain in your

Overview of LUKE

house. All grumbled about this for Zaccheus was a sinner. Zaccheus tells Jesus that half of his possessions he is giving to the poor. And if he gains anything by blackmail, he is giving back fourfold. Today salvation came to this home. *The Son of Mankind came to seek and to save the lost.*

> Lost is *apollumi* in the Greek. It is most often translated "destroyed." For those who think that "destroyed" in the Scriptures is a permanent condition from which there is no salvation ... the Son of Mankind came to seek and to save "the destroyed ones."

Parable of the nobleman and his slaves (19:11)

As Jesus nears Jerusalem, they suppose that *instantly* the kingdom of God is about to be *looming up*. He tells them of a nobleman who goes into a far country to obtain for himself a kingdom. He calls together ten of his slaves and gives to them ten minas to go into business while he is away. The nobleman's citizens hate him, and do not want him to reign over them.

When the man returns after obtaining the kingdom, he finds that the first slave had earned ten minas. *Well done!* Seeing that he was faithful in the least, this slave was given authority over ten cities. The second slave earned five minas and was given authority over five cities.

But another slave kept his mina in a handkerchief, for he feared the nobleman and saw he was a harsh man who picked up what he did not lay down, and reaped what he did not sow. *Wicked slave!* The mina was taken from him and given to the one who had ten minas.

To everyone who has shall be given. These, my enemies who are not willing for me to reign over them; slay them in front of me.

Triumphal entry (19:28)

The entire multitude of disciples rejoice, praising God with a loud voice concerning all the powerful deeds they perceived. Blessed be the King coming in the name of the Lord! Some of the Pharisees tell Jesus to rebuke His disciples. *If ever these will be silent, the stones will be crying.*

Lamenting over Jerusalem (19:41)

If you knew what is for your peace! Yet now it was HID FROM YOUR EYES. The days are coming when your enemies will surround you and level you; because YOU KNEW NOT THE ERA OF YOUR VISITATION.

> Israel's fate is now sealed. Her enemies will overcome her, and Jerusalem will be destroyed. But Israel's defeat will not be permanent. She will only be hardened and "set aside" until the full complement of nations enters, according to the words of Paul. (Romans 11:25)

Merchants cast from the sanctuary (19:45)
It is written, My house shall also be a house of prayer, yet you make it a burglars cave.

He teaches daily in the sanctuary (19:47)
The chief priests, scribes and foremost of the people seek to destroy Him. But they did not know what to do, for all the people sought to hear Him.

CHAPTER 20

Jesus' authority questioned (20:1)
As He teaches in the sanctuary, *bringing the evangel,* the chief priests and scribes question Jesus. By what authority are you doing these things? Who is giving you this authority? He replies with a question: *Is the baptism of John of heaven or of men?* Seeing this as a trap, they say that they do not know. *Neither am I telling you by what authority I am doing these things.*

Parable of the vineyard (20:9)
A man leases his vineyard to farmers and travels for a considerable time. Later he sends a slave to the farmers to collect fruit from the vineyard, but they lash the slave and send him away empty. He sends a second slave, and then a third, but they also are lashed and wounded and cast out. So the man sends his son. But the farmers reason he is the enjoyer of the allotment, and if they kill him they will gain the allotment. So they kill the son. Thereupon, the owner will be coming and destroying the farmers. What is this that is written: *The stone which is rejected by the builders, this came to be for the head of the corner.*

They seek to lay hands on Jesus (20:19)

But they are afraid of the people. So they send eavesdroppers, disguising themselves to be just, in order to trap Jesus by His words and give Him up to the governor.

They ask Him if it is allowed to give a tax to Caesar. *Be paying Caesar's to Caesar, and God's to God.* The Sadducees, who say there is no resurrection, try to entrap Jesus with questions about seven brothers who die, reminding Him that according to Moses the wife of a man who dies goes to his brother. In the resurrection, they ask, whose wife is she? *In the resurrection the dead are not marrying, and neither can they still be dying, for they are equal to messengers and are sons of God.*

They dared not ask Him anything more. He asks them, *How are some saying that the Christ is David's Son? For in the Psalms David is calling Him Lord.*

In the hearing of the entire people Jesus says to His disciples, *Take heed of the scribes, who are wanting to walk in robes, and are fond of salutations in the markets and front seats in the synagogues and first reclining places at the dinners, who are devouring the homes of widows and, for a pretense, are excessively wordy in praying. These will be getting more excessive judgment.*

CHAPTER 21

Poor widow's offering (21:1)

This poor widow casts in more than all; for she gives all the livelihood that she has.

The sanctuary will be destroyed (21:5)

As some admire the sanctuary, Jesus tells them in coming days not a stone will be left upon a stone; it will be demolished.

They ask Him what will be the sign of these days (21:7)

Be not deceived, for many will be coming in My name saying that "I am" and that the season is near.

When you hear of battles and turbulences, be not dismayed; for these things must occur first, but not immediately is the end. Nation will be roused against nation, and kingdom against kingdom. There will be great quakes, famines and pestilences. There will be fearful sights and great signs from heaven.

Overview of LUKE

But before all these things they will be persecuting you, giving you up into the synagogues and jails, and leading you off to kings and governors on account of My name. Yet this shall enable a testimony. Don't think about your defense, for I will give you words and wisdom. You will be given up by family and friends and they will put some of you to death. You will be hated by all because of My name. By your endurance will you be acquiring your souls.

Whenever you see Jerusalem surrounded by encampments, her desolation is near. Flee into the mountains and country, for these are days of vengeance to fulfill all that is written. There will be indignation on this people.

They will be falling by the sword and led into captivity into all nations. Jerusalem will be trodden by the nations until the eras of the nations may be fulfilled. There will be signs in the sun and moon and constellations. The nations will be perplexed at the resounding of the sea. There will be fear and worry of that which is coming on the inhabited earth, for the powers of the heavens will be shaken.

***AND THEN** they shall be seeing the Son of Mankind coming in a cloud with power and much glory.*

Parable of the fig tree ^(21:29)

When buds appear, summer is near. So also when you see these things, the kingdom of God is near. By no means may this generation be passing by till all *should* be occurring.

> All of these things would have occurred in their generation, had Israel repented. Jesus' statement is conditional. Their hardness resulted in a delay; a delay we will later see in Paul's writings worked to the advantage of the nations. Had Israel repented and had these events been accomplished in that day, God would not have set aside Israel and caused the nations to become joint heirs within the Body of Christ. This was a *secret* hidden for the time being, and later revealed to Paul.

Take heed, and don't be burdened with indulgence and drunkenness and the worries of life's affairs. Be vigilant, prevailing so as to escape all these things which are about to occur, and to stand in front of the Son of Mankind.

> Is the Body of Christ called to experience these things and *persevere* or *prevail*? Remember; Jesus is speaking to and about Israel. These words

Overview of LUKE

are not directed to or about us, within the Body of Christ. If we attempt to apply these words directly to ourselves in this present day, God's truth will be distorted and we will be led into confusion.

During these days Jesus teaches in the sanctuary, and at night He camps in the mount called Olivet. And the entire people come early to hear Him in the sanctuary.

CHAPTER 22

Judas agrees to betray ^(22:1)

The chief priests and scribes seek to kill Him but they fear the people. Satan enters into Judas and he meets with the chief priests and officers and agrees to betray Him. He seeks an opportunity without a throng present.

Passover ^(22:7)

Now comes the day of unleavened bread, in which the Passover must be sacrificed. Jesus sends Peter and John to make preparations. At the dinner He tells the twelve, Under no circumstances may I be eating of the Passover till it may be fulfilled in the kingdom of God. I will not drink the wine till the kingdom of God may be coming.

He serves the meal to the twelve. This is my body, given for your sakes. This do for a recollection of Me. This cup is the new covenant in My blood, shed for your sakes.

Jesus observes that the one who will give Him up is at the table. This must occur, *but woe to that man through whom He is being given up.* As the twelve contemplate this, there develops a rivalry among them as to which of them is greatest. Jesus tells them that the kings of the nations and those with authority lord it over the people, but they are different. Let the greatest among you become as the youngest. Let he who is leading be as the one serving.

And I am covenanting with you, that you may be eating and drinking at My table in My kingdom. You will be seated on thrones, *judging the twelve tribes of Israel.*

> Jesus is speaking to his disciples. In the eon to come, when He returns, they will judge the twelve tribes of Israel. We see once again that Jesus' entire message as recorded by Luke is directed to Israel and not the nations.

Overview of LUKE

Jesus points out that Satan claims men, but Simon's faith may not be defaulting. *Establish your brethren.*

> This is the charge made to Peter. *Establish your brethren.* In Acts we will see Peter do this. And we will see that Peter's letters to his brethren are also for the purpose of establishing his brethren.

Lord, with Thee I am ready to go to jail or to die. But Jesus tells him, Before a cock crows today three times you will deny knowing Me.

Jesus reminds the twelve that when they were commissioned and went out to the people, they were not to take a purse with them; and they were not in want. But now, he who has a purse let him pick it up. Let him sell his cloak and buy a sword. That which is written must be accomplished.

> Buy a sword? The time has changed. Jesus has described the events to take place upon the earth before His return. They are to be diligent, and watchful, and prepared.

At the Mount of Olives (22:39)

Be praying not to be entering into trial. He pulls away from them and prays, Father if it is Thy intention, carry aside this cup from Me. However, not My will, but Thine, be done. He sees a messenger from heaven, strengthening Him. Returning to the disciples He finds them sleeping and asks, Why are you drowsing? Rise, pray, lest you may be entering into trial.

Judas betrays (22:47)

A throng comes, led by Judas who betrays Jesus. One of the disciples smites a slave of the chief priest, cutting off his ear. *Give leave,* Jesus tells them. And He heals the man.

Daily I am with you in the sanctuary, and you do not act. But this is your hour and the jurisdiction of darkness. They lead Jesus to the house of the chief priest.

Peter denies Him (22:55)

After denying that he knows Him three times, a cock crows. The Lord looks at Peter, and Peter is reminded of the declaration Jesus had made. He laments bitterly.

Overview of LUKE

Before the Sanhedrin (22:63)

The men scoff at Jesus and lash Him. They beat His face and taunt Him to prophesy. They speak many words of blasphemy against Him. As the eldership of the people are gathered, both chief priests and scribes, they lead Jesus into their Sanhedrin. If you are the Christ, tell us.

If I should tell you, you would not be believing. From now on the Son of Mankind shall be sitting at the right hand of the power of God. Then are you the Son of God, they ask. You are saying that I am. What more do we need? We hear from his mouth.

CHAPTER 23

Before Pilate (23:1)

This man we found perverting our nation and forbidding to give taxes to Caesar, and saying he is Christ, a king. Pilate asks, Are you the king of the Jews? Jesus replies, You are saying so.

Pilate reports that he finds no fault in Jesus. But they are insistent, saying He is exciting the people. Pilate, learning Jesus is a Galilean, sends Him to Herod.

Before Herod (23:8)

Herod is overjoyed to see Jesus for he had wanted to become acquainted, having heard much about Him. He expects to see a sign. Herod inquires of Jesus but He does not answer. The chief priests and scribes strenuously accuse Him. Herod scorns Him and scoffs at Him. He clothes Jesus in splendid attire and sends Him back to Pilate.

Before Pilate again (23:13)

Having found no fault in Jesus, Pilate plans to discipline and release Him. But the people cry out for Jesus to be crucified and for Bar-Abbas, a murderer and insurrectionist, to be released. The loud voices and persistence of the chief priests and people prevail, and Pilate gives in to their will.

Crucifixion (23:26)

Jesus is led away, and Simon from Cyrene is enlisted to carry the cross. A vast multitude of the people follow, and the women who grieved over Him. *Daughters of Jerusalem, do not lament over Me. But lament over*

Overview of LUKE

yourselves and your children, for coming are days when those who are barren will be happy. They will ask the mountains to fall on them.

Father, forgive them, for they are not aware what they are doing. The chiefs say, Others he saves. Let him save himself if this is the Christ of God, the Chosen One. The soldiers also scoff at Him: If you are the king of the Jews, save yourself. An inscription is placed over Him in letters of Greek, Roman and Hebrew: The King of the Jews is this.

One of the malefactors being crucified beside Him blasphemes Jesus: Are not you the Christ? Save yourself and us. But the other rebukes the first: We justly get back the deserts of what we commit. Yet this One commits nothing. To Jesus he says; Be reminded of me, Lord, whenever Thou mayest be coming in Thy kingdom. *Verily, to you am I saying today, with Me shall you be in paradise.*

> The original Greek manuscripts contained no punctuation. Punctuation in our English translations is interpretation. Most versions render this passage: *I am saying, today you will be with me in paradise.* This supports the prevailing opinion that the one who dies goes immediately to heaven or hell. But since the Scriptures in many passages tell us that there is no consciousness in the death state, at least until the resurrection, we see that the punctuation should be placed as follows: *I am saying today, you will be with me in paradise.*

In the sixth hour, darkness came over the whole land till the ninth hour. Then the curtain of the temple is rent in the middle. Jesus shouts loudly, *Father into Thy hands am I committing My spirit.* Saying this, He dies.

The centurion, observing these things, glorifies God; Really this Man was just. All those known to Him, and the women who follow with Him from Galilee, stood afar off, observing.

Burial (23:50)

Joseph of Arimathea, a good and just man who had himself anticipated the kingdom of God, approaches Pilate and requests the body of Jesus. He places the body in a rock-hewn tomb. It was the day of preparation and a sabbath *lighted up.* The women who had followed from Galilee gaze at the tomb and see how the body was placed. They return and make ready spices and attars. But on the sabbath *they are quiet, according to the precept.*

Overview of LUKE

CHAPTER 24

Resurrection (24:1)

Early on one of the sabbaths the women and certain others come to the tomb bringing the spices they had made ready. They find the stone rolled away, and entering they see that the body of the Lord Jesus is gone. Two men appear to them in flashing attire. *Why are you seeking the living with the dead? He is not here, but was roused. Be reminded how He speaks to you, being still in Galilee, saying that "The Son of Mankind must be given up into the hands of men, sinners, and be crucified, and the third day rise."*

Returning, they report all these things to the eleven and to all the rest. But their declarations seem as nonsense and the others disbelieve. But Peter runs to the tomb and sees only the cloths, and he comes away marveling to himself.

On the road to Emmaus (24:13)

On the same day two of them walk toward Emmaus, talking with one another about all that had happened. Jesus Himself draws near to them and goes with them, but *their eyes were held* so as not to recognize Him. With a sad countenance they tell Jesus the events that had occurred. They crucify Him. Yet we expected that He is the One about to be redeeming Israel. But some of our women amaze us, telling of an apparition of messengers who say He is living.

> HE IS THE ONE ABOUT TO BE REDEEMING ISRAEL. At this point, then, the expectation is not salvation or redemption of any except ISRAEL.

Finally Jesus speaks: O foolish and tardy of heart to be believing on all which the prophets speak! Must not the Christ be suffering these things, and be entering into His glory? He goes on to interpret to them all in the scriptures which concerns Himself, beginning from Moses and all the prophets. But still they do not recognize Him.

They urge Jesus to remain with them, for it is near dusk. As He reclines with them at the table and takes the bread, blessing it, their eyes are opened and they recognize Him. *And He became unapparent to them.* Returning to Jerusalem they find the eleven and those with them, who tell the men that the Lord was seen by Simon and that He was roused. The men tell of the events that had occurred on the road.

Overview of LUKE

Jesus appears (24:36)

As they are talking Jesus appears in their midst. They are dismayed and become frightened, supposing they are beholding a spirit. Jesus says to them, Why are you disturbed? See My hands and My feet, that it is I. Touch Me and see, for a spirit does not have flesh and bones. At their still disbelieving, Jesus eats before them.

The Commission (24:44)

He opens up their mind to understand the scriptures, and says to them: *Thus it is written, and thus must the Christ be suffering and rise from among the dead the third day, and there is to be heralded in His name repentance for the pardon of sins, to all the nations, beginning from Jerusalem. Now you shall be witnesses of these things.*

I am delegating the promise of My Father on you. Be seated in Jerusalem until you should be putting on power from on high.

Ascension (24:50)

Leading them to Bethany, He lifts up His hands and blesses them, and He is carried up into heaven. Worshipping Him, they return to Jerusalem with great joy, and are continually in the sanctuary, praising and blessing God.

RECAP

What makes Luke's account unique? What can we learn from his words as to his specific purpose in writing?

1. Matthew's genealogy traces the lineage through to Joseph, the earthly father of Jesus. Perhaps this is because Matthew's objective is to show the legal qualifications are met in Jesus to be king on David's throne. But Luke's genealogy traces the lineage through to Mary, as Jesus' father is in truth God. Luke's emphasis is not on proving Jesus' legal right to the throne; but the fact that He is the Son of God. E. W. Bullinger notes that Matthew's purpose is to demonstrate that Jesus is the MESSIAH and the KING OF ISRAEL. Mark shows Jesus as God's SERVANT. Luke positions Jesus as the IDEAL MAN. In Luke, the HUMANITY of Jesus is emphasized.

2. Jesus will bring salvation to His people, the house of David. (1:57)

Overview of LUKE

3. While Jesus healed and cast out demons, the purpose of His ministry is to bring the evangel of the kingdom of God. (4:42)

4. When Jesus commissions His disciples to go out, the mission is the same. They are to proclaim: *Near to you is the kingdom of God.* (10:1)

Overview of LUKE

John

An Overview of the Scriptures, by
BOB EVELY © 2018.
An Independent Minister of Christ Jesus
Of the church at Wilmore, Kentucky

CHAPTER 1

In beginning (1:1)

Observe closely the precise words John uses in these opening lines (in the original Greek). Wherever the definite article occurs in the Greek we will insert the English "the" (it is ignored in most translations for readability). And wherever the definite article is absent we will insert the indefinite article [a].

> *In [a] beginning was the word,*
> *And the word was toward the God,*
> *And [a] God was the word.*
> *This was in [a] beginning toward the God.*
> *All came into being through it, and*
> *Apart from it not even one thing came into being which has come into being.*

This passage is often used to support the "trinity" doctrine, allegedly demonstrating that God and Christ are the same. But consider where the definite article appears and where it is absent. *The word* points toward *the* God, but is not *the* God itself. The word (Christ) is *[a] God*.

Keep in mind that God (*theos* in the Greek; *el* or *elohim* in the Hebrew) is a *title* that means *subjector*. God the Father is <u>The</u> God, the <u>Supreme</u> God, but He is not the only God (subjector) spoken of in the Scriptures. Consider the following passages in the Old Testament where *elohim* (subjector) is used of men.

- Exodus 7:1 - Moses is appointed as *elohim* to Pharoah
- Exodus 21:6; 22:8,9 - *Elohim* is translated "judges"
- Psalm 82:1 - God judges the *elohim* (so the elohim cannot be God)

And consider the following instances in the New Testament where *theos* refers to others besides *The* God.

- John 10:34 - Is it not written in your law that 'I say you are *gods*.'
- 1 Corinthians 8:5-6 - Many *gods* and many lords, but for us there is one ...
- 2 Corinthians 4:4 - the *god* of this eon blinds ...
- Philippians 3:19 - whose *god* is their bowels ...

Overview of JOHN

2 Thessalonians 2:4 - there are those 'termed a *god*'

Think about the opening words of Genesis. God spoke (words) and things came into being. He said let there be light; and there became light. Here in John we see *word* and *light* being used symbolically of Christ. God spoke and the Word (Christ) came into being. Everything that was subsequently created came into being through Christ. (Colossians 1:16) Representative of light, He appeared in the world of darkness but the darkness *grasped it not*.

John the Baptist is commissioned by God ... (1:6)

to testify concerning the light *that all should be believing through it.*

> So the *purpose* of the coming of the light (Christ) is to cause men to BELIEVE.
>
> Observe that John provides no genealogy and no birth narrative. After a brief introduction he immediately proceeds to the ministry of John the Baptist. His purpose in writing obviously does not require a genealogy as did the accounts of Matthew and Luke.

The true light is coming into the world ... (1:9)

enlightening every man. But the world, which came into being through Him *knew Him not.* He came *to His own,* but they did not accept Him. But those who are believing in His name were begotten of God, and He gives them the right to become children of God. The Word became flesh and lives among us.

> He came to enlighten EVERY MAN. To accomplish this He begins with "His own" (ISRAEL), His chosen people, intending that through Israel ALL men will be blessed and enlightened. (Genesis 12:3; 22:18; 26:4; 28:14)
>
> A word about "THE TRINITY" ... Christ is *begotten* of God the Father. He then becomes God's agent in creating all other things. (Colossians 1:16) As I study the Scriptures apart from human tradition as much as is possible, I have come to believe that the doctrine of the "trinity" is not biblical, but is a fabrication of man. I do not believe that God the Father and Christ Jesus the Son are the same "person." I believe that Christ Jesus is *lesser* than God the Father, as Jesus Himself states on many occasions. But I believe that Christ Jesus is high above all other created beings. I do not believe it is proper to argue about the "trinity" or other

Overview of JOHN

beliefs concerning the personhood of God and the personhood of Christ. The scriptures never tell us we must become versed on this doctrine or make it a primary subject of our teaching or proclaiming. It seems to me if one believes that God the Father and Christ Jesus the Son are the same *person* within the "God-head," or if one believes that Christ Jesus the Son is the firstborn of creation, distinct from God the Father yet high above all else that is created, the difference is not really that large. Is Christ divine? Yes; for He was fathered supernaturally by God's spirit. But He is not the same *person* as God the Father; He is the *SON* of God. The important thing is that we study the Scriptures and gain our understanding from that which God has revealed, and not from the traditions and teachings of men that have been passed down to us.

John the Baptist gives his testimony (1:15)

The law came through Moses; grace and truth through Jesus Christ. No one has ever seen God; but the *only-begotten God unfolds* Him.

> Note the two Gods that John mentions. THE God that no one has ever seen, and the only begotten God that unfolds or reveals Him.

The priests and Levites approach and ask John who he is. *I am the voice of one imploring, In the wilderness straighten the road of the Lord! according as said Isaiah the prophet.* [from Isaiah 40:3] As he sees Jesus coming, John proclaims, *Lo! the Lamb of God Which is taking away the sin of the world! ... That He may be manifested TO ISRAEL I came baptizing in water.*

> Observe closely; He is taking away the sin of THE WORLD, but at this stage of God's unfolding plan Jesus is being manifested TO ISRAEL. (1:31)

This is He Who is baptizing in holy spirit. I have seen and have testified that this one is the Son of God.

> This is John the Baptist's testimony; that Jesus Christ is the *Son of God*, and that He is being manifested to Israel. Throughout John's account we will be introduced to a series of testimonies, all with the intent of demonstrating Jesus is the *Son of God* and to cause BELIEF in this One Who has been sent and commissioned by THE God.

Overview of JOHN

Jesus gathers the disciples ^(1:35)

Two of John's disciples leave and follow Jesus. One of them (Andrew) goes and finds his brother Simon and tells him they have found the *Messiah which is being construed Christ*. Jesus tells Simon, *You shall be called Cephas, which is being translated Peter*. He also calls Philip to follow. Philip finds Nathanael and tells him he's found the One Whom Moses wrote about in the law and the prophets; Jesus from Nazareth. When Jesus makes a prophetic observation concerning Nathanael, he responds: Thou art *the Son of God; the King of Israel*.

CHAPTER 2

He turns water into wine ^(2:1)

This beginning of the signs Jesus does in Cana of Galilee, and manifests His glory, and His disciples believe in Him.

> This is the first sign (miracle) and it has resulted in the disciples BELIEVING in Him. So we see the purpose of the signs and wonders Jesus performs is TO CAUSE BELIEF.

He casts merchants from the sanctuary ^(2:13)

Do not be making My Father's house a house a merchant's store. His disciples are reminded that it was written, *The zeal of Thy house will be devouring Me.* [see Psalm 69:9]

The Jews ask what signs He will show them. *Raze this temple, and in three days I will raise it up.* The Jews disbelieve, thinking He is speaking of the physical temple; but He is speaking *figuratively* concerning His body. Later, when He is roused from among the dead, His disciples are reminded of His words, *and they BELIEVE the scripture and the word which Jesus said.*

> Observe that as we study the Scriptures we need always to consider; is this to be taken literally or figuratively? The Jews interpreted Jesus' words literally, but He intended His comments to be taken figuratively. Some will insist we are always to interpret the Bible literally unless that is not possible, and only then to interpret figuratively. But we see here that this man-made rule is not always correct, and can lead to a misunderstanding of what God has revealed.

Overview of JOHN

More signs ^(2:23)

At the Passover many believe in His name, beholding the *signs* that He did. But Jesus did not entrust Himself to them, *for He knew what was in mankind.*

> Think about Jesus' comment concerning mankind. Man was created in God's image, but after Adam's disobedience man inherited a mortal, dying body with a propensity to sin. Jesus comes to bring redemption and reconciliation with God. Man left to his own devices is wicked and unrighteous, contrary to the opinion of many humanists and philosophers. Without God's grace *none* would be righteous and *none* would even seek God. (Romans 3:10)

CHAPTER 3

Nicodemus – You must be born again ^(3:1)

Nicodemus, a Pharisee and a chief of the Jews, approaches Jesus. We are aware that You are a Teacher come from God, for no one can be doing these signs if God should not be with Him.

If anyone should not be begotten of water and of spirit, he cannot be entering into the kingdom of God. ... You must be begotten anew.

> *You* (plural) must be *begotten anew* ("born again"). Jesus is speaking not of Nicodemus as an individual, but ISRAEL. Israel is anticipating the Messiah and the restoration of the kingdom, and must be "born again" to enter it.

> This passage is not directed to the Body of Christ or to the world at large. It is directed to ISRAEL. Israel must be "born again" to be ready for the kingdom that is to be restored upon the earth. The Body of Christ is not commanded to be born again; we are a *new creation.* (2 Corinthians 5:17; Galatians 6:15) We are not told we must BECOME a new creation; we are MADE TO BE a new creation. It is all God, not human effort.

No one has ascended into heaven except He Who descends out of heaven, the Son of Mankind.

> As the firstborn of creation, Christ has existed in the heavenly realm since the very beginnings of creation. Now He descends out of heaven to manifest (make known) THE God.

Overview of JOHN

As Moses exalts the serpent in the wilderness, thus must the Son of Mankind be exalted, that everyone believing on Him should not be perishing, but may be having life eonian. For thus God loves the world, so that He gives His only-begotten Son, that everyone who is BELIEVING in Him should not be perishing, but may be having LIFE EONIAN.

> While God loves THE WORLD and sent His Son to bring life, during the time of Christ's earthly visitation He directs His message TO ISRAEL, as Israel is prepared for the kingdom's restoration. He is telling those of Israel what they must do to enter the kingdom and have life in the coming EONS when it is restored. Since the days of Abraham, God has intended to bless ALL mankind. He has a plan to accomplish this, comprised of a progressive order of events. (Genesis 12:3; 22:18; 26:4; 28:14)

God does not dispatch His Son into the world that He should be judging the world, but that the world may be saved through Him. He who is believing in Him is not being judged; yet he who is not believing has been judged already, for he has not believed in the name of the only-begotten Son of God.

> All men start out as unbelieving and are judged against God's standard of righteousness and found wanting. None are righteous. None are seeking God. (Romans 3:10) Every man is helpless without God's intervention, and this intervention comes with Christ Jesus and begins with Israel. Those of Israel who believe, and who obey based upon that belief, will no longer be judged; for Christ, the only-begotten of God, has intervened on their behalf.

Light has come into the world, and men love the darkness rather than the light, for their acts were wicked ... and they are not coming to the light, lest his acts may be exposed.

Jesus baptizes in Judea (3:22)

> We are told in 4:1 that Jesus Himself is not baptizing, but His disciples.

The disciples of John the Baptist question John; for all are now going to Jesus to be baptized. John replies, A man cannot get anything if it should not be given him out of heaven. ... He must be growing, yet mine it is to be inferior. He Who is coming from above is over all. ... The Father is loving the Son and has given all into His hand.

God's indignation or life eonian (3:36)

He who believes in the Son has *life eonian*, but he who is stubborn as to the Son shall not be seeing life but *the indignation of God is REMAINING on him*.

> Take note of a very key word; REMAINING. As stated earlier, all men apart from God are found wanting and God's indignation is on them. We will see this indignation in active form in Revelation. But for now God introduces a solution; His only-begotten Son. Those who believe will have life in the kingdom upon the earth in the eons to come, but for those who are stubborn and who do not believe God's indignation REMAINS on them and they will not enjoy life within the kingdom when it is restored.
>
> Later God will introduce a more "global" solution; once Israel's stubbornness causes her to be temporarily set aside (Romans 11:25) and reconciliation is offered to men of ALL nations without preference to Israel. Then God will require faith alone, and not faith PLUS obedience (works) as is the case when John records his account. But in the era of Jesus' visitation upon the earth, God is speaking to ISRAEL in preparation for the kingdom's restoration upon the earth.

CHAPTER 4

The Samaritan woman (4:1)

Leaving Judea and heading into Galilee, Jesus passes thru Samaria. He asks a Samaritan woman for a drink and tells her, If you were aware of the gratuity of God and Who it is Who is saying to you Give Me a drink, you would request of Him and He would give you *living water*. The One who drinks of this living water *shall under no circumstances be thirsting for the eon*. The water will become in him a spring of water, welling up into *life eonian*.

> Observe the words LIFE EONIAN. Not "eternal" life, but life for the EON or EONS to come ... within the restored kingdom.

The woman recognizes that Jesus is a prophet and tells Him, Our fathers worship in this mountain, but you say that one must worship in Jerusalem. *Coming is an hour when neither in this mountain nor in Jerusalem shall you be worshiping the Father*.

> Jesus is introducing a change. No longer will the emphasis be upon worshipping in Jerusalem on specific feast days. Worship will not be

exterior at all, but in spirit and truth. In our day worship is no longer about going to a place ... not to Jerusalem ... not to a temple or synagogue ... and not to a church.

Salvation is of the Jews. But coming is the hour, and now is, where the true worshipers will be worshiping the Father in spirit and truth. God is spirit, and those worshiping Him must WORSHIP IN SPIRIT AND TRUTH.

> Observe: SALVATION IS OF THE JEWS! (4:22) Salvation is extended to the nations, but only through Israel; until Paul later introduces a new revelation from God ... Israel and the nations as joint-heirs with no preference or distinction.

The woman tells Jesus that when the Messiah comes, the One called Christ, He will inform them of all things. Jesus replies, *I am He.* She returns to the city and proclaims that she met a man who tells her all that she did. *Is this not the Christ?*

The disciples ask Jesus to eat but He replies, My food is that I should be *doing the will of Him Who sends Me,* and should be *perfecting* His work. I commission you to reap that for which you have not toiled. Others have toiled, and you have entered into their toil.

Many Samaritans believe because of the woman's testimony. At their request Jesus stays with them for two days, and many more believe because of His word while He is with them. *We are aware that this truly is the Saviour of the world, the Christ.*

> The testimony of the Samaritan woman and those who hear her proclamation is that Jesus is the Saviour of the world; the Christ.

Healing a nobleman's son (4:45)

Jesus comes again into Cana of Galilee and encounters a nobleman whose son is about to die. Jesus tells the man, *If you should be perceiving signs and miracles, you should under no circumstances be BELIEVING.*

> Jesus is continually asked to heal, but HIS COMMISSION IS NOT TO BRING HEALING. It is to cause BELIEF as the restoration of the kingdom approaches.

The man again asks Jesus to come, lest the boy dies. Jesus tells the man, Go; your son is living. When the man learns that his son had been healed in the very hour that Jesus gave the word, he and his whole house BELIEVE.

CHAPTER 5

Healing on a sabbath ^(5:1)
Jesus goes to Jerusalem for a festival of the Jews, and heals a man by the sheep gate pool. *You have become sound. By no means longer be sinning, lest something worse may be coming to you.*

> Sinning has consequences. Jesus always shows compassion and often brings healing and forgiveness, but His message is also to *stop sinning*.

The Jews criticize ^(5:10)
Since it is a sabbath the Jews object to the man picking up his pallet. They persecute Jesus and seek to kill Him, claiming He *annulled the sabbath*. And by saying His Father is God He makes Himself *equal* to God.

> They did not think Jesus claimed to be the same *person* as God. But by claiming to be God's Son they felt He was espousing to be *equal* in stature with God.

The Son can only do what the Father gives Him to do ^(5:19)
The Son cannot do anything of Himself. But as the Father is *rousing the dead and vivifying*, so also the Son is *vivifying whom He will*. He who is not honoring the Son is not honoring the Father Who sends Him. He who hears my word and believes Him Who sends Me has *life eonian* and is not coming into judging. God gives the Son *authority to do judging* since He is a son of mankind. The hour is coming when all who are in the tombs shall hear His voice, and those who do good shall go out into a resurrection of *life*, yet those who commit bad things into a resurrection of *judging*.

> Notice that life after the resurrection at this point is based on WORKS; not faith alone as Paul would later proclaim. Remember; God is executing His plan in stages in a progressive order.

My judging is just, for I am not seeking My will, but the will of Him Who sends Me.

I am saying these things that you may be saved.

The works which I am doing are testifying concerning Me that the Father has commissioned Me.

Overview of JOHN

> Again we see that His works; the signs and healings; are done to testify as to His authority and His commission from the Father. He seeks to have them BELIEVE.

But you are not believing and not willing to come to Me that you may have life. You have not the love of God in yourselves. You get glory from one another and are not seeking glory from God. If you believed Moses you would believe Me, for He writes concerning Me.

CHAPTER 6

Feeding 5000 (6:1)
A vast throng follows Jesus because they see the signs He does on the sick. He feeds 5000 men who observe: This truly is *the Prophet* Who is coming into the world.

He walks on the sea (6:15)
Knowing they are about to make Him king, Jesus retires alone into the mountain. The disciples board a ship without Him to cross the sea to Capernaum. A storm arises and the disciples see Jesus walking on the sea.

Work for food that remains (6:26)
When a throng gathers Jesus tells them, Do not work for food that is perishing, but for food that is remaining for *life eonian* which the Son of Mankind will be giving to you. *This is the work of God, that you may be* BELIEVING *in that One Whom He commissions.*

> He was sent from heaven, commissioned by God, and proclaimed the kingdom to be restored unto Israel. All that He says and does is to cause BELIEF, and righteous works in accord with belief.

Bread of life (6:30)
They ask for a sign, reminding Jesus of the manna that was provided to their ancestors in the desert. He replies, My Father is giving you bread out of heaven, the bread that is descending out of heaven and giving life to the world. *I am the Bread of life.* He who is coming to Me will not be hungering. He who is coming to Me I will not cast out.

Not My will, but the Father's will (6:38)
I have descended from heaven not to do My will, but the will of Him Who sends Me. This is the will of My Father; that everyone who

Overview of JOHN

beholds the Son and BELIEVES in Him may have *life eonian*, and I will be raising him in the last day.

> BELIEF results in LIFE EONIAN; life in the eons to come when the kingdom is restored upon the earth.

Some cannot believe (6:41)

The Jews murmur, Is not this Jesus, the son of Joseph, with whose father and mother we are acquainted? How is he saying that out of heaven have I descended?

> They stumbled because of their pre-conceived notions concerning the Christ. Surely the Christ could not be someone they have known since childhood. They COULD NOT BELIEVE because of this stumbling block.

NO ONE CAN COME *to Me if ever the Father Who sends Me should not be* DRAWING *him.* (6:44)

> Remember; none are righteous. None are seeking God. (Romans 3:10-12) If the Father did not DRAW men to Himself, none could come. Christ is His means of doing this, and He BEGINS WITH ISRAEL.

THE God has not been seen (6:46)

The Father has not been seen by anyone except by the One Who is from God. This One has seen the Father.

> God the Father has never been seen. He is spirit. He is manifested to man by His Son, Christ Jesus, the *image* of God. (Hebrews 1:3) The Trinity doctrine contends that the Father, Son and Holy Spirit are three-in-one. But God the Father IS spirit. How, then, can the Father be one part of the "God-head" and the Holy Spirit another? Additionally this passage speaks of two distinct entities; God Who has never been seen, and another Who is *from* God.

Believing = life eonian (6:47)

He who is *believing* in Me has *life eonian*. I am the living Bread that descends out of heaven. Anyone eating of this Bread shall be living *for the eon. The spirit is that which is vivifying. The flesh is not benefiting anything.* The declarations which I have spoken to you are spirit and are life. But there are some of you who are not believing.

Overview of JOHN

Some cannot come (6:65)
NO ONE CAN BE COMING TO ME, IF IT SHOULD NOT BE GIVEN HIM OF THE FATHER.

> No amount of human will and determination can cause one to believe in Christ if it is not given by the Father. The Father desires that ALL men be saved (1 Timothy 2:4) but His plan is to draw (not force; but *draw*) all men thru a progression of events. All that we see in the Scriptures and in our world today is a work in progress that is leading to the point when God's will is finally accomplished and He becomes All in all. (1 Corinthians 15:22-28) During the time of Jesus' earthly visitation it is ISRAEL that plays a part in God's unfolding plan, and even among Israel some are given to believe while others *cannot* believe.

Many disciples turn away (6:66)
With this, many of His disciples turn away and walk with Him no longer. But Simon Peter declares, We believe and know that Thou art the Holy One of God. Jesus replies, Do not I choose you, the twelve, and one of you is an adversary?

> Jesus chose even one who is an adversary. The adversary, too, will play a part in God's unfolding plan.

CHAPTER 7

Jesus teaches at the Feast of Tabernacles (7:1)
Jesus walks in Galilee and not in Judea, for the Jews seek to kill Him. His brothers encourage Him to go to Judea. If you are doing these things, manifest yourself to the world. They do not believe in Him. Jesus replies, *My season is not yet present.* The world hates Me for I am testifying that its acts are wicked.

> MY SEASON IS NOT YET PRESENT. (7:6) At times we think God should act in a certain way to correct some difficulty or to prevent some calamity. These thoughts are always centered on our own perspective and desires. But perhaps in these times His season is not yet present. Still; all will be well in the end as God is in control and His ultimate will cannot be thwarted.

Jesus does go to the festival, but as in hiding. Midway through the festival He goes into the sanctuary and teaches. The Jews marvel, How is this one acquainted with letters, not having learned? Jesus replies, My teaching is not Mine but His Who sends Me. He who is speaking

Overview of JOHN

from himself is seeking his own glory, but He Who is seeking the glory of Him Who sends Him, this One is true, and injustice is not in Him.

I AM FROM HIM, AND HE HAS COMMISSIONED ME. (7:29)

They seek to arrest Him, but no one lays a hand on Him for His hour had not yet come. Many of the throng believe in Him. The Christ, whenever He may come, will not do more signs than what this Man does.

> *Again we see that the signs were for the purpose of authenticating Jesus and prompting belief.*

Still a little time am I with you, and I am going away to Him Who sends Me. And where I am, there you cannot be coming. The Jews wonder where He is about to go that they will be unable to follow.

Schism (7:37)

On the last, the great day of the festival Jesus stands and cries, If anyone should be thirsting, let him come to Me and drink. Some of the throng observe, This truly is the Prophet. Others, This is the Christ. There came to be a *schism* amongst the throng. Nicodemus says to his fellow-Pharisees, No law of ours is judging a man, if ever it should not first be hearing from him and know what he is doing. But the Pharisees object, noting that no prophet has ever come from out of Galilee.

CHAPTER 8

Woman caught in adultery (8:1)

Jesus returns to the sanctuary and teaches. The scribes and Pharisees lead to Him a woman caught in adultery. In the law, Moses directs us that such are to be stoned. What are you saying? They were looking for a way to accuse Him. He replies, Let the sinless one of you first cast a stone at her. He then says to the woman, I am not condemning you. Go. From now on by no means any longer be sinning.

> *How often this episode is referenced, but only partially. Many are quick to point out that Jesus does not condemn the woman, but they fail to remember the second part of his message – Go and sin no more. The fact that He refuses to condemn the woman does not mean that "anything goes." There are behaviors that are acceptable to God, and behaviors that are not.*

Overview of JOHN

Light of the world (8:12)
I am the light of the world. The one who follows should not walk in darkness but will have *the light of life*. The Pharisees criticize, saying Jesus' testimony is not true. Jesus reminds them that in the law the testimony of two men is true. I am the One testifying concerning Myself, and the Father Who sends Me is testifying concerning Me.

> If the Father and the Son are one being as the Trinitarian doctrine claims, here we would have the testimony of only one, not two.

I am going away and you will be seeking Me, and in your sin shall you be dying. Where I am going you cannot be coming. You are of that which is below. I am of that which is above. You are of this world. I am not of this world. If you should not be believing in Me that I am, you shall be *dying in your sins*.

> Belief is necessary for those of Israel hoping to enter the kingdom when it is restored. BELIEF is what Jesus is looking for as He proclaims and demonstrates His authority with signs and wonders.

> *Dying in your sins* is not a permanent condition. It will prevent those not believing from enjoying life in the restored kingdom in the age/eon to come, but it will not exclude them from the final reconciliation of all when God becomes All in all. (1 Corinthians 15:28)

Jesus does not proclaim His own message (8:26)
What I hear from Him, these things I am speaking to the world. From Myself I am doing nothing. As My Father teaches Me, these things am I speaking.

Many believe in Him (8:30)
He says to the Jews who believe, If you remain in My word you are truly My disciples. You will know the truth, and the truth will be making you free. The one doing sin is a slave of sin.

> Jesus is speaking TO THE JEWS who believe and who REMAIN in His Word.

Some object – Abraham is our father (8:39)
If God were your Father you would have loved Me. For out of God I came forth and am arriving. Neither have I come of Myself, but He commissions Me. You are of your father, the Adversary. He was a

Overview of JOHN

mankiller *from the beginning*. Truth is not in him. He is a liar. I am speaking the truth, and you are not believing Me.

The Jews say that Jesus is a Samaritan and has a demon. I have no demon, but I am honoring My Father, and you are dishonoring Me. If anyone should be keeping My word he should under no circumstances be beholding death *for the eon*.

> Those among Israel who do not believe and keep His word will remain dead when the kingdom is restored. They will not enjoy eonian life during that period of time. Still, all will ultimately be reconciled to God at the end of the eons (1 Cor 15:22-28) for it is God's will that ALL be saved (1 Timothy 2:4) and He is operating ALL in accord with the counsel of His will. (Ephesians 1:11)

Ere Abraham came into being, I am. They pick up stones to cast at Him, but He was hidden from them and passed through their midst.

CHAPTER 9

Jesus heals a blind man (9:1)

His disciples ask, Who sinned, this man or his parents that he should be born blind? Jesus replies, Neither; but it is that the works of God may be manifested in him. The man is healed on a sabbath day.

Some of the Pharisees claim that Jesus cannot be from God, for He is not keeping the sabbath. But others observe, How can a man who is a sinner be doing such signs? There develops a *schism* among them.

The healed man tells the Pharisees, Unless this Man were from God, He could not be doing anything. Jesus later encounters the man and asks, Are you believing in the Son of Mankind? The man replies, I am believing, Lord. And he worships Him.

> The testimony of the man who was healed: Jesus is the Son of Mankind. And when the man *worships* Him, he does so one-on-one and in the place where he is. No temple, synagogue, church, assembly, music, singing or anything else is needed. The man simply *worships* on his own and where he is. Study the word *worship* throughout the Scriptures and you will find that is simply means to *come-toward* the object of worship, whatever form that may take.

CHAPTER 10

Overview of JOHN

The Shepherd (10:1)

The shepherd is the one who is entering through the door. The shepherd calls his own sheep by name and leads them out. They are acquainted with his voice. They flee from the voice of an outsider.

I am the Door of the sheep. If anyone should be entering through Me, he shall be *saved*, and shall enter and find pasture. I came that they may have *life eonian*, and have it superabundantly.

> Saved = saved from death in the eon to come. The one saved will enjoy life in the kingdom when it is restored.

I am the ideal Shepherd Who lays down his *soul* for the sake of the sheep. A hireling sees the wolf coming and flees. I have other sheep that are not of this fold. Those also I must be leading. There will be one flock, one Shepherd.

Schism among the Jews (10:22)

A *schism* arises among the Jews because of His words. They surround Him in the sanctuary and ask, If you are the Christ, tell us with boldness.

I told you and you are not believing. The works I am doing in the name of My Father, these are testifying concerning Me. But you are not believing, as you are not of My sheep. My sheep I am giving *life eonian*. They will not be perishing *for the eon*.

> So *the works I am doing* (the healings and other miracles) are for the purpose of TESTIFYING concerning Him, to result in BELIEF.

> Concerning those who are not His sheep ... it is not because they refuse to believe. They do not believe because they are not His sheep. Remember; no one can come to Him (believe) unless the Father draws them. (6:44; 6:65) One day ALL will believe and will be reconciled to God. But in His progressive plan, at the moment some CANNOT believe. This, too, is a part of His plan.

I and the Father are One (10:30)

I and the Father are one. Hearing these words, the Jews intend to stone Him. You, being a man, are making yourself God. Jesus replies, Is it not written in your law that I say you are gods? Yet you say I am blaspheming, having said Son of God am I.

Overview of JOHN

> Jesus is not claiming to be THE God. He is distinct from and lesser than God the Father. He is COMMISSIONED by the Father. He carries out not His own agenda but that of the Father. He is not THE God but A God, the SON of God.

If I am not doing My Father's works, do not believe Me. But if I am doing them, believe the works that you may be knowing and believing that the Father is in Me, and I am in the Father.

> Again we see the purpose of His works ... to cause BELIEF. He came not to heal. The healings and other miracles are for the purpose of authenticating Him as the Son of God and the One commissioned by God; to cause BELIEF.

He comes along the Jordan, near the place where John had baptized. MANY NOW BELIEVE because of the signs He has performed and the things John had taught concerning Him.

> And once again we see that the testimonies given throughout John's account (in this case John the Baptist) and the signs Jesus has performed have caused in some the desired effect; BELIEF.

CHAPTER 11

Lazarus raised from the dead (11:1)

Lazarus is infirm and his sisters, Mary and Martha, send for Jesus. He replies, This infirmity is not to death but for the glory of God, that the Son of God should be glorified through it. Jesus delays for two days before going to Bethany.

He tells his disciples, Lazarus our friend has found repose, but I am going that I should be awakening him out of sleep. Upon arriving in Bethany they learn that Lazarus had died and had been in the tomb for four days. Martha laments, Lord, if Thou were here my brother would not have died. But even now I know that whatever you request of God, He will be giving to Thee.

Your brother will be rising.

I am aware that he will be rising in the resurrection in the last day.

I am the Resurrection and the Life. He who is believing in Me, even if he should be dying, shall be living. And everyone who is living and believing in Me should not be dying *for the eon*. Are you believing this?

Yes, Lord, I have believed that Thou art the Christ, the Son of God.

> Before proceeding, Jesus verifies that His works and the testimonies to this point have caused Martha to BELIEVE.

Jesus tells them to remove the stone from the tomb. He prays, Father, I thank Thee that Thou hearest Me. I say this that they should be believing that Thou commission Me.

> So His desired effect in what happens next is to cause those observing to BELIEVE that He has been commissioned by God.

With a loud voice He commands Lazarus to come forth. Many of the Jews who observe BELIEVE in Him. Yet some of them come away to the Pharisees and tell them what Jesus has done. The chief priests and Pharisees worry that with these signs *all will be believing in him, and the Romans will come and take away our place as well as our nation.*

> Here we see why the Jewish leaders fear Jesus. They stand to lose their "place;" their position of stature. And they fear that the elevation of Jesus will cause the Romans to take away their freedom to function as a nation.

Caiaphas, the chief priest at that time, notes that it is expedient that one man should die for the sake of the people and not the whole nation perish. And from this day the chief priests and Pharisees plan to kill Him.

> Caiaphas unknowingly prophesies that Jesus would die for the sake of the nation, and that He would gather the scattered children of God into one. Those of Israel who have been scattered into other nations are the "other sheep" Jesus had referred to earlier.

CHAPTER 12

Mary anoints His feet (12:1)

Six days before the Passover Jesus comes to Bethany and attends a dinner with Lazarus, Martha and Mary. Mary rubs His feet with precious attar, and Judas Iscariot criticizes. The attar could have been sold and the money given to the poor. Judas appears to be concerned for the poor, but he was not, for he was a thief.

Let her be, that she should be keeping it for the day of my burial. For the poor you have always with you, yet Me you have not always.

Overview of JOHN

Triumphal entry (12:12)

Hearing that Jesus is coming to Jerusalem a vast throng prepares to meet Him. They shout, Hosanna! Blessed is He Who is coming in the name of the Lord! and The King of ISRAEL!

Jesus finds a little ass to ride, as it had been written, Do not fear, daughter of Zion! Lo! your King is coming, sitting on an ass's colt. His disciples do not know this at the time, but when Jesus is later glorified they are reminded of these things that had been written of Him. Those who observed Jesus when He roused Lazarus testify to the throng, so they hear this sign that Jesus had done.

Jesus foretells His death (12:23)

The hour has come that the Son of Mankind should be glorified. If a kernel of grain, falling into the earth, should not be dying, it remains alone. But if it should be dying, it brings forth much fruit. He who is fond of his soul is destroying it, and he who is hating his soul in this world shall be guarding it for *life eonian*.

Now My soul is disturbed. Shall I ask the Father to save Me from this hour? For this I have come to this hour. Father, glorify Thy name! Now is the judging of the world. Now shall the Chief of this world be cast out. And I, if I should be exalted out of the earth, shall be drawing ALL to Myself.

> Observe closely these words. Speaking of His impending crucifixion; I SHALL BE DRAWING ALL TO MYSELF. (12:32) What permits us to interpret ALL as just those who believe in this lifetime? He does not say "all who believe" but simply ALL.

The throng considers that in the law the Christ remains for the eon. How, then, can He say the Son of Man must be exalted (crucified)?

Still a little time the light is among you. Be walking while you have the light, lest the darkness may be overtaking you. Be believing in the light, that you may be becoming sons of light.

They could not believe (12:37)

But after having done so many signs before them, they did not believe in Him. THEY COULD NOT BELIEVE, seeing that Isaiah said *He has blinded their eyes and callouses their heart, lest they may be perceiving with their eyes, and should be apprehending with their heart, and may be turning about.* [from Isaiah 6:9,10]

Overview of JOHN

> And so BELIEF is not something that one can simply develop through perseverance and effort. It is clearly stated here that some COULD NOT BELIEVE as their eyes had been blinded. As God's progressive plan unfolds, some will believe and give testimony to others; while others CANNOT believe. But all is a work in progress leading to the point when one day ALL will believe and will be reconciled to God, for this is His desire and plan. (1 Timothy 2:4; Ephesians 1:11)

Many of the chiefs *did* believe in Him, but because of the Pharisees they did not avow it for they would have been put out of the synagogue. They love the glory of men rather than the glory of God.

> As a side note, it is interesting that many in the church today are locked within the mindset of their church leaders. If truth is found in the Scriptures that is outside the bounds of the teachings of one's church they risk being *put out* of the church if they speak out. This is especially true of church leaders and those leading Christian organizations, universities, etc. They are often locked in error because they wish not to be *put out* by questioning the creeds or statements of faith particular to their brand of Christianity. Often it is because *they love the glory of men rather than the glory of God.*
>
> I was once told that creeds and orthodoxy protect the truth from heresy. I have come to find that creeds and orthodoxy lock men into error that has been espoused and preserved by the traditions of men.

I came not to judge (12:47)

If any should be hearing My declarations and not be maintaining them, I am not judging him, for I came not that I should be judging the world, but that I should be saving the world. He who is repudiating Me and not getting My declarations has that which is judging him. The word that I speak will be judging him in the last day, seeing that I speak not from Myself, but the Father Who sends Me.

> There will come a day of judging. But that too will be a part of God's progressive plan, leading toward the ultimate reconciliation of ALL.
>
> 1. None are righteous.
>
> 2. None are even seeking God.
>
> 3. Jesus comes; the Son of God and commissioned by God.

- 140 -

4. God enables SOME to believe and give testimony.

5. Judgment is coming upon those not believing, but with the same goal of leading to belief ... because it is God's will that ALL men are saved ... and He is working ALL in accord with the counsel of His will.

CHAPTER 13

Jesus washes the feet of His disciples (13:1)

It was before the Passover festival, and the Adversary was already cast into the heart of Judas. Jesus washes the feet of the disciples. He tells them this is an example. You also ought to be washing one another's feet.

He foretells His betrayal (13:18)

I am aware whom I choose, but that the scripture may be fulfilled, He who is eating bread with Me lifts up his heel against Me. I am speaking to you before it is occurring, that you should be believing, whenever it may be occurring, that I am. One of you will be giving Me up. The disciples are perplexed.

He it is to whom I, dipping in the morsel, shall be handing it. He dips the morsel and hands it to Judas, and Satan enters into him. But none of the disciples understand, and they do not know Judas' purpose as he leaves.

A new precept — love (13:34)

A new precept I give you; *be loving one another* as I love you. By this all shall be knowing that you are my disciples.

He predicts Peter's denial (13:36)

Where I am going you cannot follow Me now, yet you shall be following subsequently. Peter objects, saying that he will lay down his life for the Lord. But Jesus tells him before a cock crows he will deny Him three times.

CHAPTER 14

He comforts the disciples (14:1)

I am going to make ready a place for you. And if I should be going, I am coming again and I will be taking you along to Myself, that where I am you also may be. I am the Way and the Truth and the Life. No one is coming to the Father except through Me.

> Some claim that to believe God will ultimately save all is to discount the need for Christ. But NO ONE can come to the Father except through Christ. Without Christ NO ONE would be saved. But because of Christ NO ONE will ultimately be lost. To see God's plan to ultimately save all is not to discount the work of Christ. Rather, the work of Christ is magnified and given its full credit when one realizes the full implications.

He who has seen Me has seen the Father. Are you not believing that I am *in* the Father and the Father is *in* Me? I am going to the Father. And whatever you should be requesting in My name, this I will be doing, that the Father should be glorified in the Son. If you should ever be requesting anything of Me in My name, this I will be doing.

> Remember; Jesus is speaking only to those of Israel, and only at this particular time as God's overall plan unfolds. Many today espouse the "name it and claim it" theology based on passages such as this. But to do so is taking Scripture out of context and is an attempt to *steal* things given only to Israel and only in this past era.

If you should be loving Me you will be keeping My precepts.

I shall be asking the Father and He will be giving you another consoler to be with you *for the eon* – the spirit of truth.

I will not leave you bereaved; I am coming to you. Seeing that I am living, you also will be living.

He who has My precepts and is keeping them is loving Me. If anyone should be loving Me, he will be keeping my word, and My Father will be loving him, and We shall be coming to him and making an abode with him.

The consoler, the holy spirit which the Father will be sending in My name, will be *teaching* you all and *reminding* you of all that I said to you.

> This is Jesus talking with His disciples at this particular time. His disciples will be taught directly by the holy spirit, and those things will then be recorded in the Scriptures and preserved for later generations. It is the Scriptures that provide us with God's teachings today, not supernatural teachings given directly by the holy spirit. That was a different era. Later we will read that Paul <u>completed</u> the word of God,

Overview of JOHN

(Colossians 1:25) and it is to the Word of God we must turn for teachings in our present era.

My peace I am giving to you. Not according as the world is giving to you, am I giving to you.

CHAPTER 15

The Grapevine (15:1)

I am the true *Grapevine*. Every branch that brings forth no fruit He is taking away. Every branch bringing forth fruit He is cleansing, that it may be bringing forth more fruit. A branch cannot be bringing forth fruit from itself, if it should not be remaining in the grapevine.

You are the *branches*. Apart from Me you can do nothing. If anyone should not be remaining in Me he was cast out as a branch and into the fire. If you should be remaining in Me and My declarations should be remaining in you, whatever you should be wanting request, and it will be occurring to you. In this is My Father glorified, that you may be bringing forth much fruit.

Greater Love (15:9)

Greater love than this has no one, that one may be laying down his soul for his friends. You are My *friends*. No longer am I calling you slaves. All that I hear from My Father I make known to you.

The disciples are commissioned (15:16)

You did not choose Me, but *I chose you*, and I appoint you to be going away and bringing forth much fruit, and your fruit may be remaining.

Be loving one another. If the world is hating you, know that it hated Me first. If they persecute Me, they will be persecuting you also, as they are not acquainted with Him Who sends Me.

If I had not come and spoken to them, they would have no sin. But now they have no excuse concerning their sin. They have seen Me and hated Me.

You are testifying, seeing that you are with Me from the beginning.

> Here we see the purpose of His disciples. They were with Him from the beginning of His earthly ministry, and they testify to what they have seen and heard. All of this is preserved for us today in the Scriptures.

CHAPTER 16

Overview of JOHN

The disciples will face affliction (16:1)
They will be putting you out of the synagogues. Coming is the hour when they will be killing you, supposing they are offering divine service to God.

The consoler will be sent (16:5)
It is expedient for you that I may be going away. If not the consoler would not be coming to you. I will send him to you and that will expose the world concerning sin, righteousness and judging.

Still much I have to say to you ... (16:12)
but you are not able to bear it at present. When the spirit of truth comes it will be guiding you into all the truth ... informing you. These things I have spoken to you that in Me you may have peace. In the world you have affliction. But take courage; I have conquered the world.

> The disciples were not ready to hear more at this point, but it would later be revealed to them and they would record these new truths in their epistles, which are now preserved for us in the form of the Scriptures.

CHAPTER 17

Jesus prays for disciples, present and future (17:1)
Father the hour has come. I glorify Thee on the earth, finishing the work which Thou hast given Me. Glorify Me, Father, with the glory that I had before the world is with Thee.

> Christ did exist in the heavens before being dispatched to earth. He was the firstborn of God's creation, and He served as God's agent in all subsequent creation. (Colossians 1:16) He then emptied Himself and took on the form of man, as commissioned by God (Philippians 2:5-8) that He might redeem mankind and reconcile ALL unto God, in accord with God's desire and plan.

Concerning those whom Thou hast given Me, no longer am I in the world but they are in the world. Keep them in Thy name, that they may be one as We are. I have given them Thy word, and the world hates them. Keep them from the wicked one. They are not of the world, as I am not of the world. But not concerning these only am I asking, but also concerning those who are believing in Me through their word that they may all be one, as Thou art in Me, and I in Thee ... that the

Overview of JOHN

world should be believing that Thou dost commission Me ... that they may be one as We are One.

> It is not that God the Father and Jesus Christ the Son are one in the same person. They are *one* in the same way that all believers are *one*.

Thou lovest Me before the *disruption* of the world. They know that Thou commissioned Me, and I have made known to them Thy name.

CHAPTER 18

Jesus is arrested (18:1)

Jesus enters a garden with His disciples. Judas comes with a squad, and with deputies of the chief priests and Pharisees. Peter draws a sword and strikes off the ear of the chief priest's slave.

Thrust the sword into the scabbard. The cup which the Father has given Me, may I not be drinking it?

> Peter had the best of motives. He sought to protect His Lord at all costs. But he acted from his own perspective and his own plan in a fleshly manner. He is rebuked because His quick physical response is counter to the spiritual plan that is unfolding. Let us not be quick to act in the flesh from our own perspectives even if we have the best of motives and intentions, lest we find ourselves at odds with God's unfolding plan.

They apprehend Jesus. Peter follows, along with another disciple. Before a cock crows, Peter denies that He knows Jesus three times.

Before Pilate (18:29)

Pilate addresses the Jews, Take him and judge him according to your law. But they reply that it is not allowed for them to kill anyone. Pilate turns to Jesus. You are the king of the Jews? Your nation and the chief priests give you up to me. What is it you do?

My kingdom is not of this world. If my kingdom were of this world, My deputies would have contended, lest I be given up to the Jews. But *now* My kingdom is not hence. You are saying that I am a king. For this I have come into the world; to be testifying to the truth.

> While His kingdom is not *of* this world (i.e. it is of God), it will be established upon the earth as it was in David's day. *But NOW My kingdom is not hence.* The time has not yet come.

Pilate turns to the Jews. I am not finding one fault in him. Offering to release one prisoner in the Passover, the Jews choose Bar-Abbas, a robber, instead of Jesus.

CHAPTER 19

Pilate scourges Jesus. The soldiers place a wreath of thorns on His head, a purple cloak on Him, and slap Him. The chief priests and deputies clamor: Crucify him. According to our law he ought to die, for he makes himself son of God.

Pilate is afraid. He says to Jesus, Are you not aware that I have authority to release you or to crucify you?

No authority have you against Me in anything, except it were given to you from above.

The Jews clamor, Everyone who is making himself king is contradicting Caesar. We have no king except Caesar. Pilate gives Him up to them, that He may be crucified.

Crucifixion (19:17)

They lead Him to a placed called a Skull's Place, which in Hebrew is Golgotha. They crucify Him along with two others. Jesus cries out, It is accomplished. And reclining His head, He gives up the spirit.

John's testimony (19:35)

He who has seen has testified, THAT YOU SHOULD BE BELIEVING. These things occurred that the scripture may be fulfilled.

> This is John's summary and his purpose in writing. He has provided the testimony of many throughout his account, and now he provides his own eyewitness testimony and his conclusion. He *believes*, and has written that his audience (Israel) will also BELIEVE.

Burial (19:38)

Joseph of Arimathea, a disciple of Jesus yet secretly for fear of the Jews, asks Pilate for the body of Jesus. Accompanied by Nicodemus he gets the body, binds it in swathings with spices, and place it in a new tomb in the garden.

CHAPTER 20

Overview of JOHN

Resurrection (20:1)

On *one of the sabbaths*, Miriam Magdalene comes to the tomb in the morning and finds that the stone has been removed. She races back to Simon Peter and another disciples (of whom Jesus was fond) and they race to the tomb. They see the swathings lying there. The other disciple sees and believes, for not as yet were they aware of the scripture that He must rise from the dead.

> As noted in Matthew's account of the resurrection, *one of the sabbaths* is often erroneously translated "the first day of the week," giving the notion that the resurrection occurred on a Sunday. But there is no linguistic warrant to render the translation in this way. It is only carelessness and the contamination of the Scriptures by religious tradition.
>
> There is nothing found here in the Greek for "first," or "day," or "week." The problem is the thinking that *Sabbath* always refers to the weekly Sabbath (Saturday), but Leviticus 23 summarizes seven festivals/feasts that are referred to as *special Sabbaths*. Some Sabbaths occur in close proximity. For example, on the tenth day of the seventh month we have the Day of Covering (Atonement) and five days later is another Sabbath; the Festival of Ingathering. The *evening of the Sabbaths* is where an evening ends one Sabbath and begins another. Occasionally a festival falls on the weekly Sabbath, in which case we have a double Sabbath, or *the day of the Sabbaths*. When we see the phrase *one of the Sabbaths* it refers to the series of Sabbaths between Wave Sheaf and Pentecost. In 28:1 we have just concluded Passover a few days earlier, and *one of the Sabbaths* would seem to refer to the regular weekly Sabbath; a Saturday.
>
> In reality it matters not the day on which the Resurrection took place. The FACT that Christ was resurrected is the key; not the particular day it happened. *One, indeed, is deciding for one day rather than another day, yet one is deciding for every day. Let each one be fully assured in his own mind.* (Romans 14:5)

As Mary stands outside the tomb, two messengers ask, Woman, why are you lamenting? She sees Jesus but is not aware it is He, supposing that He is the gardener until Jesus calls her by name. She replies, Rabboni, which means teacher.

Go to My brethren and tell them I am ascending to My Father and your Father, my God and your God. Mary returns and reports to the disciples, I have seen the Lord.

That evening, though the doors are locked because they fear the Jews, He appears in their midst, and the disciples rejoice. As the Father has commissioned Me, I am sending you. He exhales and says to them, Get holy spirit. If you should be forgiving anyone's sins, they have been forgiven them.

Thomas doubts (20:24)

Thomas had not been with them when Jesus appeared. The other disciples tell him, We have seen the Lord, but Thomas will not believe *should I not perceive in His hands the print of the nails, and thrust my hand into His side.*

Eight days later Jesus appears again and says to Thomas, See My hands, and thrust your hand into My side. Thomas replies, My Lord and My God.

Seeing that you have seen Me, you have believed. Happy are those who are not seeing and believe.

> # Consider the lesson learned from Thomas!

Thomas is an example of those who do not believe by faith. Are they to be discarded and sent to an eternity of torment? Thomas would not believe UNTIL he saw for himself. He was not rejected for his failure to believe by faith. True, it is preferred that we believe by faith. *Happy are those who are not seeing and believe.* But those who do not ... who CANNOT believe ... will one day see the Lord face to face. And they, like Thomas, will then believe. Will they be rejected for their failure to believe by faith in their lifetime when they had ample opportunity? Look to Thomas for the answer to that question.

Overview of JOHN

Why John writes (20:30)

Jesus does many other signs in the sight of His disciples which are not written in this scroll. *Yet these are written that you should be believing that Jesus is the Christ, the Son of God, and that, believing, you may have life eonian in His name.*

> This very clearly states John's purpose in writing; that his audience (Israel) should BELIEVE that Jesus is the Christ, the Son of God, and thereby have *life eonian*, or life in the kingdom when it is restored upon the earth in the eons to come.

CHAPTER 21

Jesus appears to Peter (21:1)

Jesus manifests Himself to His disciples at the sea of Tiberias. Peter had gone fishing but had caught nothing. Jesus stands on the beach, but the disciples do not know it is Him. He tells them, Cast the net on the right side of the ship. They do so and catch a multitude of fish. The disciples whom Jesus loved says to Peter, It is the Lord.

Jesus says to Peter, Graze My lambkins ... shepherd My sheep ... graze My little sheep. When you were younger you girded yourself and walked where you would; yet whenever you may be growing decrepit you will stretch out your hands and another will be girding you and carrying you where you would not. He said this signifying the death with which he would be glorifying God.

Peter asks concerning the apostle that Jesus loved, Lord, what of this man? Jesus replies, If I should be wanting him to be remaining till I am coming, what is it to you? You be following Me.

> Let us not ask why we seem to have it worse than another. We serve our Lord as He determines. That is our only concern.

RECAP

What makes John's account unique? What can we learn from his words as to his specific purpose in writing?

John clearly states his purpose. "These are written that you should be BELIEVING that Jesus is the Christ, the Son of God, and that, believing, you may have LIFE EONIAN in His name." (20:30)

John presents many testimonies. John the Baptist, the Samaritan woman, the Samaritans, Moses, Peter, the blind man that was healed, Martha. His account is a succession of testimonies of the authenticity of Jesus; the fact that He is the Son of God and that He was sent by and commissioned by God. This is what John's audience is to BELIEVE; that He was sent by God and commissioned by God. (7:29)

All of these testimonies, and the many signs that Jesus performed, were presented for the purpose of causing BELIEF. And let us not forget that throughout John's account his words are directed to ISRAEL and not to those of the nations. This does not mean God is not interested in the welfare of ALL mankind. But at this point in time, in accord with His progressive and unfolding plan, He is working with Israel.

Summary

An Overview of the Scriptures, by
BOB EVELY © 2018.
An Independent Minister of Christ Jesus
Of the church at Wilmore, Kentucky

While each of the four gospel writers had a singular purpose, let us now consider the four in total. What are some things we can discern from these four accounts of the Lord's visitation to the earth?

To Israel

Numerous times we see that the group being addressed is exclusively Israel. Jesus tells the Canaanite woman He was not commissioned except for the lost sheep of Israel. (Matthew 15:24) When He commissions the Twelve He tells them to go only to the lost sheep of Israel. (Matthew 10:6) At this point in God's unfolding plan, He is working with Israel. It is a grave mistake to steal these things spoken only to Israel and only in this particular era, and this mistake will lead to great error in our understanding of what God has revealed.

The restoration of the kingdom

What is taking place in the era of Christ's visitation is readying Israel for the kingdom that is to be restored upon the earth, with Christ reigning. It is the kingdom established by God that David once ruled over, and now the scattered kingdom awaits her king to return. John the Baptist's message was, Repent for near is the kingdom. (Matthew 3:2) When Jesus began preaching and teaching it was the same message. (Matthew 4:17)

Belief (faith) + works is called for

All that Jesus says and does is for the purpose of causing BELIEF. And with belief there is also an expectation of works. Unlike a later time when Paul will proclaim to those of all nations, "Faith alone," during the era of Christ's visitation upon the earth we hear the call for faith plus works as the requirement for entering the restored kingdom.

Life eonian

What is at stake here is life eonian … life in the kingdom when it is restored upon the earth. Those not exhibiting faith plus works among

Summary

Israel will not enjoy life in these coming eons. Still, they will not be left out when God accomplishes His ultimate goal ... the salvation and reconciliation of all when He becomes All in all. (1 Corinthians 15:28)

It is a huge mistake to carelessly render *aionian* in the Greek as eternal. It is eonian; a period of time with a beginning and an end. And only when we observe this correct translation of the word can we recognize God's ultimate plan.

He came not to bring healing, but to cause BELIEF

Belief is the key. This is why Jesus healed and performed miracles; to authenticate the fact that He is the Son of God and that He was sent and commissioned by God.

Throughout the four gospel accounts we see a distinctive Jewish focus. We find many Old Testament references. Jesus announces the restoration of the kingdom. But the king and the kingdom are rejected by the Jews who so anxiously awaited their coming, and the king is crucified.

Still, the evangel remains the same in the book of Acts when Peter (who was given the keys to the kingdom) proclaims the same message. Christ has been crucified and resurrected, but in the book of Acts it is still the kingdom to come upon the earth that is being proclaimed, and it is proclaimed exclusively to the Jews as was the case throughout Matthew. Salvation, or life in the eon to come, is life in the kingdom of the heavens when it comes upon the earth with Christ upon the throne. But again throughout Acts we see the evangel of the kingdom rejected. When the kingdom is *finally* rejected at the end of Acts, the Jews (and the kingdom evangel) are set aside for a season and the uncircumcision evangel is declared to Jew and Gentile alike without distinction or preference. But have the Jews lost their chance? Has "The Church" taken their place? Paul tells us that Israel has been calloused UNTIL *the complement of the nations may be entering,* after which time *all Israel shall be saved.* (Romans 11:25)

The gospels tells us of a time when the kingdom to come upon the earth was proclaimed to the Jews. Acts continues that message, even after the death and resurrection of Christ. As Acts ends Paul tells us that a new evangel is going out to Jew and Gentile alike. But when this present age has ended the kingdom evangel will once again be proclaimed upon the earth, and we see this happen in Revelation.

Index

All, I shall be drawing	139
All things possible	41, 72
Believe, some could not	139-140
Beginning, in [a]	121
Born again (Nicodemus)	125
Commission (purpose) of Jesus	61, 85
Commission of the Twelve	23, 91
Death, what happens at	24
Divorce	40, 71
Ecclesia (church)	33-4
Emmaeus, Road to	117
End times	46, 75, 106, 107, 111
End times, no one knows day/hour	48
Eon, the coming	27, 72
Eonian chastening	49
Eonian fire	37
Eonian life	41, 72, 94, 108, 127
Evangel	18, 81
Evangel of the kingdom	17, 47, 60, 61, 89
Figurative vs, literal	33, 124
Gehenna	19, 24, 38
Great Commission	47, 53, 77
Greatest command	45
Hades	26
Healing	18, 22, 23
Hell (Gehenna)	19, 24
Indignation	127
Indignation, impending	15-16, 84
Israel, David's coming kingdom	73
Israel, only to	23, 32, 68

Israel, the God of	82
Israel, upon twelve thrones judging	41, 113
John 3:16	126
Keys to the kingdom	33-4
Kingdom	15
Kingdom, keys to	33-4
Kingdom locked	29, 34, 46
Lord's Prayer	20, 95
Lost (apollumi)	109
Lost sheep, parable	38, 102
Marriage	71
Miracles	18, 21-22, 23, 25, 30, 66, 94
None can come unless drawn	26, 94, 131, 132
Parables	28-29, 30, 64, 89
Paradise, you shall be with me	116
Pardon	39, 106
Pardon, 70 x 7	39
Pharisees, woe to	45, 97
Prayer, ask and receive	74, 95
Reign of Christ for the eons	82
Resurrection	45
Resurrection of Jesus	52, 77, 117, 147
Rich Man & Lazarus	103
Rightly dividing	7
Satan, get behind me	69
Saved	41, 66, 136
Sermon on the Mount	19, 25, 87
Sheep and goats	49
Snares	37, 71, 106
Soul	70, 73
Sound words, a pattern of	6
Thomas doubts	148

Tradition of the Pharisees	31, 67
Trinity	76, 122-3, 129, 131, 136-7, 145
Tyre & Sidon would have repented	25, 93
Unpardoned sin	27, 63, 97
Upon this rock	33
Visitation, era of	110
Worship	32, 65, 127, 135

This overview contains the thoughts and opinions of the author and is a work in progress as his study of the Scriptures continues. Some things that God has revealed are very clear. That Christ died for our sins; that He was entombed; and that He was roused (1 Corinthians 15:3) is clear. That all are to be ultimately reconciled to God thru the work of Christ is also very clear (1 Corinthians 15:20-28). But on many specifics in the Scriptures there are a variety of interpretations and opinions, and none should conclude they have the complete and final understanding on these matters that are less clear. The reader is encouraged to consider various opinions, but to study and to think for himself. Within the Body of Christ we should study and discuss our understandings so as to mutually reach a more complete understanding of that which God has revealed.

Unless otherwise noted, Scriptures are taken from the Concordant Literal New Testament and the Concordant Version of the Old Testament. Concordant Publishing Concern, 15570 West Knochaven Road, Santa Clarita, CA 91387 (www.Concordant.org)

Grace Evangel Fellowship:
P O Box 6, Wilmore, KY 40390
www.GraceEvangel.org

About the Author

Bob Evely is Vice President with a national company, overseeing sales, sales training, servicing, marketing, and special projects. He is a graduate of Oakland University (Rochester, Michigan) and has a Master of Divinity (M.Div.) Degree from Asbury Theological Seminary (Wilmore, Kentucky). For three and a half years Bob served as pastor of the Canton and West Point United Methodist Churches in Salem, Indiana; and for five years he served as pastor of the Open Door Free Methodist Church in Nicholasville, Kentucky. Both were bi-vocational positions, with Bob supporting his family through full time employment.

In May 2002 Bob resigned as pastor of Open Door Free Methodist Church to found Grace Evangel Fellowship, an independent ministry/church based in Wilmore, Kentucky. His ministry includes writing, speaking, teaching, and corresponding via email.

Bob resides in Wilmore, Kentucky with his wife Jill (since 1975). Originally from the Romeo, Michigan area the Evelys have five children: Cris (Jen), Dusty (Sharon), Chad (Molly), Kari (Jason), and Scott (Martha). As of this writing they are blessed with 7 grandchildren (Elinor, Allison, Abby, Lilli, Livi, Annabelle, and Alex).

Jill homeschooled all five children, and for 20 years represented Sonlight Curriculum as a consultant. Besides staying busy as a wife, mother, and grandma, Jill is an accomplished soap maker (PrairieKari.com) and she continues to encourage parents interested in homeschooling their children.

The author can be contacted at Grace Evangel Fellowship, P O Box 6, Wilmore, Kentucky 40390; or via email bob@GraceEvangel.org

Books by Bob Evely

At the End of the Ages; the Abolition of Hell (2002)

The Visitation; An Overview of the New Testament, Part One (2018)

The Waiting; An Overview of the New Testament, Part Two (2018)

The Pause; An Overview of the New Testament, Part Three (2018)

The Return of the King; An Overview of the New Testament, Part Four (2018)

Many shorter writings can be found at GraceEvangel.org

Book Artists at Work
Allison, Elinor & Lilli Evely

www.ingramcontent.com/pod-product-compliance
Lightning Source LLC
Chambersburg PA
CBHW051801040426
42446CB00007B/464